THE
NEW
ENGLISH
COOKERY

THE NEW ENGLISH COOKERY

RICHARD CAWLEY

FOREWORD BY

JOSCELINE DIMBLEBY

PHOTOGRAPHS BY
TREVOR RICHARDS

OCTOPUS
BOOKS

To Andrew

Notes All recipes serve 6 people unless otherwise stated. Ovens should be preheated to the specified temperature. All spoon measures are level, unless otherwise stated. All herbs used are fresh, unless otherwise stated. Only freshly ground black pepper is used, unless otherwise stated. Follow one system of measures – they are not interchangeable. All recipes are illustrated in full colour on the pages either preceding or following them.

Note to Australian readers All measures in this book are in metric and imperial. It is important to note that the Australian tablespoon has been converted to 20 ml, which is larger than the tablespoon used in this book, and therefore 3 level teaspoons should be used where instructed to use 1 tablespoon. Kitchen scales may be used to follow either the metric or imperial columns but only one set of measures should be followed as they are not interchangeable.

A Ridgmount book

First published 1986 by Octopus Books Limited
59 Grosvenor Street, London W1

ISBN 0 7064 2612 6

© 1986 The Festival Press Limited
© 1986 Text Richard Cawley
© 1986 Photographs Trevor Richards

This book was designed, edited and produced by
The Festival Press Limited
5 Botts Mews, London W2 5AG

Filmset in Great Britain by Lineage Limited, Watford, Hertfordshire.
Colour origination by Hong Kong Graphic Arts Limited, Hong Kong.
Printed by Leefung Asco Printers Limited, Hong Kong.

Acknowledgements The Festival Press Limited and Richard Cawley would like to thank the following individuals for their contributions to this book: Christopher Corr for the full-colour illustrations; John Woodcock for the technical drawings; Susan Kinsey and Michael McGuinness for all other illustrations; Norma MacMillan, copy editor; and Ian Hands for invaluable assistance in cookery and photography sessions.

CONTENTS

FOREWORD

by JOSCELINE DIMBLEBY

Soon after Richard Cawley won the 1984 Observer/Mouton Cadet competition he invited me to lunch. My first taste of his intriguing smokey topaz chicken, the recipe for which is in this book and which he was trying out for the first time that day, assured me that Richard has a very special way with food. He was apologetic because he thought that the pudding, a delicate little timbale of wild strawberries, was not quite right. I could find no fault with it and the taste was wonderful. It soon emerged that we felt very much the same about food and cooking.

Like me, Richard is not a chef but a private cook. He wants to share his creative flair for food with everyone, not just an élite collection of gourmets. In this, his first book, he shows us that it needn't be too time consuming, too expensive or require too much skill to produce new and exciting dishes. His advice on shopping and on the final appearance of the food is inspiring and yet sensible too. There are some extremely useful pages of information and tips, clear and relevant. With his talents as a designer Richard knows just how to present a meal and make food look its best but he stresses that the taste must come first. The result is a rare combination of beautiful food which isn't too grand and tastes delicious.

Every one of the recipes is interesting and often strikingly original. Helpfully arranged into three-course menus both Richard and the photographer Trevor Richards have worked together to present them in tantalizing photographs. Yet it is a book to be used, not simply looked at; like his food Richard's cookery book is both practical and pleasing to the eye.

Everytime I read one of his recipes I think 'what a wonderful idea, I wish I had thought of it'.

Jacqueline Drinkley

INTRODUCTION

Britain has always been a melting pot for the cultures of the widely differing peoples who have settled here. Today we can witness the way that this has influenced and continues to influence every aspect of our modern lifestyle. The gradual change in our food and eating habits down the centuries illustrates a particular effect of these influences. Since long before Sir Walter Raleigh introduced us to the potato, English cooks have accepted and adopted foreign foods and ideas on cooking. The new English cookery has not yet completely emerged, but is taking shape in the minds and saucepans of many ingenious and original home cooks, and it is from the domestic kitchen rather than from the restaurants of famous chefs that the phoenix of English cookery is arising.

The time is coming when we will be rid of the reputation that has inspired so many jokes about the awfulness of English food.

English food has not always had a terrible reputation. Before the Industrial Revolution, English food was varied, imaginative and highly flavoured. The English cook, from cottage or castle, had made full use of a wide variety of herbs and flavourings, and the English herb garden became justly famous. In the country, even the poorest families had been able to grow a few herbs and vegetables, and keep some chickens and a pig. The new, urban, working-class housewife had little access to good fresh ingredients, and intense poverty and long working hours meant that there was no money or time to cook other than simply prepared dishes from meagre ingredients.

In this century, two world wars and the de-pression of the 1930s did little to rekindle an interest in creative cookery. The 1950s and 60s brought new wealth and the leisure to enjoy it – which also provoked a growing fascination with convenience foods. Already popular in the United States, tinned, frozen or processed foods made cooking quick, easy and colourful for a generation of housewives whose memories of wartime austerities were still fresh. Why make a stock, sauce or stuffing when everything can be found in a tin, cube or packet, was the message.

In the late 1950s, however, books written by Elizabeth David began to be published. Kitchens once more filled with the aromas of French country cooking. Garlic, herbs, spice and simple fresh ingredients – the everyday larder of French housewives – were redis-covered and enjoyed. Many more excellent cookbooks followed, written by fine English cooks who helped us to look back and redis-cover a forgotten heritage of traditional English recipes, and directed us to look abroad at the exciting cookery of other lands.

Modern writers on food constantly warn against the ill effects on our health from eating processed food containing chemical preserva-tives, flavourings and colourings; and from overindulging in animal fats, dairy produce and sugar. We have become aware that what we eat affects the way we feel, look and be-have. This is one of the major factors con-tributing to the rapid change in the eating habits of the English. To be conscious of eating only what is healthy is no longer considered to be cranky, but is quite commonplace. Indeed, even packaged food is evidence of the revolution – sugar-free tinned fruit, and labels declaring the contents of the tin, jar or packet to be free of chemical additives can be found on most supermarket shelves.

Foreign influences on our food have become part of everyday life. Indian and Chinese restaurants thrive, and even humble cafes display menus containing pasta and rice dishes. Scampi has settled down happily next to 'ploughman's lunch' as part of 'traditional' English pub food. This English attitude of willingness to sample, appreciate and assimilate dishes from other cultures is a major factor contributing to the present exciting state of English food.

Our shops and supermarkets supply the new ingredients we need to cook the food of people who have settled in the British Isles. New techniques of cooking have been introduced and easily learned, such as stir-frying with the help of a Chinese wok. Once we have mastered some of these techniques and dishes from other lands we do not need to stick to precise recipes. It can be great fun to experiment and try unusual combinations of ingredients and translate them into new, perhaps simpler, dishes. For example, the Chinese never eat uncooked vegetables, but beansprouts make a delicious addition to a salad in their raw state.

All over the world, ideas about food and cooking are changing rapidly and radically. This is perhaps most noticeable in the fashionable, French *nouvelle cuisine*. This style of cooking is deliciously light and decorative, using new and original combinations of good, fresh ingredients. At its best, it is almost an art form. Unfortunately, when this style of cooking is copied by lesser cooks, the results can leave the tastebuds a little confused and the stomach decidedly empty. The recipes themselves are often too daunting to attempt at home, as they require scarce and expensive ingredients. The methods are sometimes lengthy and seem too complicated for cooks without professional training. The new English cookery, however, while undoubtedly looking for fresh combinations of flavours and new ways of presenting food, takes full advantage of well-loved, easily available and inexpensive ingredients, and no dish in this book is too complicated for an inexperienced cook to try. Even *nouvelle cuisine*, although original in many ways, is still a 'variation on a theme', having its roots firmly in the tradition of classic French cookery.

New English cookery, therefore, is an amalgamation of many influences: knowledge of cooking from our own past; ideas and techniques borrowed from other cultures; the desire to eat well, either for our health or for the enjoyment of fresh ingredients unsullied by chemical additives; and the pleasure to be gained from serving delicious food with style.

Richard Cawley

SHOPPING AND NATURE'S LARDER

Shopping well is the first and most important step towards producing delicious meals. A wise cook will gather ingredients not just from one source but from a wide variety of shops, ranging from roadside stalls to giant supermarkets, looking for the best and cheapest. Choosing the freshest ingredients with which to prepare a meal is far more important than any other aspect of good cooking. A few fresh, perfect ingredients, carefully chosen and simply prepared, can make a superb and memorable meal. On the other hand, a collection of tired ingredients, past their prime, will never taste other than that, however elaborately prepared and exotically spiced they might be. It is therefore essential to take time when shopping, to find the right supplier for each ingredient and never accept less than perfect goods.

Supermarkets are often the best, most convenient and cheapest places to buy many goods. Freshness and quality can usually be relied on because of the very fast turnover of produce in these large stores. Whereas it might seem a little more romantic to buy from a small family grocer, not only may this be more expensive, but frequently goods are well past their best after sitting on the shelf for far longer than the supermarkets would allow. Even dry goods like flour, rice and pulses go stale if kept too long, and herbs and spices in packets and jars quickly lose their flavour after a few months of storage. For this reason it may be a mistake to buy in bulk, even if the saving in money makes this kind of shopping attractive. It is a false economy if eventually stale goods must be thrown away.

It is a good idea always to keep an eye open in the supermarket for new ingredients, such as free-range eggs, a fresh variety of vegetables or different wines. Many more unusual or exotic ingredients can be found in the larger supermarkets and these are often much lower in price than the same product bought in a delicatessen. So before you are tempted into some enticing little 'specialist' shop – to buy fresh pasta, dried mushrooms, vanilla pods or whatever – check first that your local supermarket doesn't have the same thing better, fresher and cheaper.

Supermarkets can be a wonderful source of high quality, inexpensive wines and spirits. Wine writers often place supermarket wines at the top of their lists of rating for quality and value. 'Own brand' wines and spirits are particular bargains, often being pounds cheaper and indistinguishable in taste from those with famous labels.

Although meat and fish can be excellent in supermarkets, it may be preferable to buy these from a butcher or fishmonger. Once you get to know your chosen supplier you will be able to rely on him for those little extra services which most supermarkets cannot supply – filleting a fish, ordering something special, or preparing a piece of meat in a different way. A little honest flattery will go a long way and will benefit your shopping, so always remember to thank your butcher if he has supplied you with a particularly good piece of meat, or your fishmonger if he has sold you some especially fine fresh fish. Likewise your supplier should only thank you if you point out that something you have bought from him was perhaps not up to the very high standard you have grown used to with his goods.

Your greengrocer must be cultivated in the same way. If he doesn't already stock some fruit or vegetable you might need, ask him and he will often try to get it for you. Also, never be afraid to ask exactly how fresh something is. Although certain things like peaches, melons and avocados are purposely picked early to finish ripening in the shop or on your kitchen window sill, most vegetables and fruits begin to deteriorate from the moment they are picked. Much 'fresh' produce on sale, particularly many foreign goods, will be perhaps three days old before you buy it. It is, therefore, sometimes preferable to serve a frozen vegetable if only less than perfect fresh ones are available. Frozen vegetables are usually frozen almost immediately after picking, and when cooked will certainly taste fresher than

Markets are enjoyable and usually cheap places to shop all over the world. Local, seasonal produce is enticingly arranged and fresh.

an unfrozen vegetable which has been stored for several days. Certain vegetables such as peas, broad beans and spinach react better to the freezing process than others like sprouts and cauliflower which are not so successful.

For those lucky enough to have a regular market, this can be the cheapest, best and most enjoyable place to shop, particularly for fruit and vegetables. Stallholders buy daily from the wholesale suppliers and try to sell as much of their goods as possible by the time they shut up shop for the day. Stalls which specialize in only a few different goods are often much cheaper than those with a wider variety because, by buying in bigger quantities, they can buy at a cheaper price, and pass their saving on to you.

Among the many other interesting places to shop for food, don't be afraid to explore Chinese, Asian, Greek and other shops which specialize in foreign produce. Shopkeepers are usually more than happy to supply information about and even recipes for unfamiliar ingredients.

Even if you don't normally frequent health food shops, take a look again. Modern health food shops sell not only brown rice and herbal teas, but can also be an invaluable source of delicious fresh ingredients. They will often stock excellent goods supplied by small individual producers – vegetables (often organically grown and particularly tasty), hand-made cheeses, honeys, home-made pickles and preserves.

Roadside stalls can also be an excellent place to buy really fresh vegetables, particularly in small out-of-the-way places. Beware, however, on big main routes. 'Fresh farm eggs' does not mean that they are free-range, and be careful that the apples you buy are really from an English orchard and not from a box with 'Cape' printed on the side.

Wherever possible it is best to get into the Continental habit of shopping daily, particularly for fruit and vegetables, and only buying enough for immediate needs. Time spent shopping can be saved when cooking. Really fresh vegetables need little preparation, and with the enormously varied selection now available for most of the year one need never tire of vegetables simply steamed or boiled.

A carefully planned shopping list is an un-

doubted help but must never be a dictator. It would be foolish to insist on buying cauliflower as you had planned if only second-rate ones were available, particularly as you might instead see some tiny fresh carrots or the first asparagus of the season.

Don't be afraid to supplement your shopping with occasional raids on 'nature's larder'. For example, all those beautiful blackberries that grow wild by the wayside could be sitting in your freezer, ready to provide luscious pies and puddings in mid-winter, yet it is surprising how few people still enjoy the delightful autumn pleasure of 'going blackberrying'. There are many more delicious foods growing wild in the countryside if one only cares to look for them. Wild food does not necessarily even involve a trip into the countryside. Even 'townies' can enjoy a creamy soup made from young nettle tops in spring or a tangy salad of tiny dandelion leaves, or taste the difference a handful of ripe elderberries can make to a simple apple pie.

Such treats are, of course, only occasional. For more everyday fruit and vegetables the guaranteed way to enjoy absolute freshness is to 'grow your own'. Young vegetables, picked only minutes before cooking, can have no equal. Not all of us have a garden large enough to accommodate rows of potatoes, carrots and onions, but even the smallest garden can be persuaded to produce something delicious for the kitchen. Runner beans look almost as pretty as their less useful cousins, sweetpeas, growing up against a small garden fence. And for those with no more than a tiny backyard or balcony, a grow-bag will provide a wonderful summer supply of fresh tomatoes.

A window box full of herbs will provide a little taste of home produce for most of the year. Even inside window-ledges can provide the perfect environment in an unreliable climate for pots of that most delicious of sun-loving herbs – basil. Even the tiniest quantity of home-grown produce, be it only a sprinkling of window-ledge herbs added to a plain omlette, will give immeasurable pleasure to both cook and guest.

The recipes in this book use mostly inexpensive, well-known and easily available ingredients. Those that may be less familiar are explained in the list on pages 28-36.

HEALTH AND FITNESS

'An apple a day keeps the doctor away.' This maxim is still sound common sense as apples contain valuable dietary fibre and vitamin C, but we now realize it is insufficient advice.

Health and fitness have become very important today, and we are constantly being told how to be healthier and live longer. Strenuous exercise, like jogging and aerobics, became quite a fad for a while, and there seemed to be a new 'miracle' diet every week. Among health addicts, fitness became almost a religion.

As is often the case with new crazes, a few extremists came to grief: poisoning from too much carrot juice or heart attacks as a result of jogging. It is most unwise for anyone, at any age, to change their diet radically and suddenly, or to exchange a routine of relative inactivity for one of regular violent exercise, without first seeking expert medical guidance.

Wisely, though, we are all gradually changing our eating habits. Because the food we eat directly affects our state of mind and body, better eating can only result in better health.

What is healthy eating? Though medical opinion sometimes differs on small points, most doctors and scientists are unanimous on certain major points.

Firstly, we must eat less. Most of us, particularly in the West, eat far more than we need. The body only requires a certain amount of fuel. Excess energy produced by excess food will be either wasted or turned into fat.

Secondly, many of us eat far too much of the wrong kinds of foods. Unlike the 'apple a day' advice, 'Drinka Pinta' now no longer seems quite such a sensible idea because we should be reducing our consumption of fatty dairy products. Experts feel that an excess of these fats plus the kinds of harmful saturated fats which are abundant in certain red meats can cause a build up of cholesterol in the body, and possibly lead to heart attacks.

The other danger is sugar. Of this we undoubtedly eat far too much. Although our bodies need a certain amount of sugar, this can be absorbed simply from eating a sensible amount of fruit and vegetables. Sweetness is definitely an addictive habit which can be broken, as those who once took sugar in tea and have given it up can attest.

The healthy diet that reduces the consumption of saturated fats and sugar should concentrate on the foods that are good for us – fish and poultry and lots of fresh vegetables and fruit. And all food should be as near its natural state as possible, with as little processing, preservatives or additives as you can find.

Following a healthy diet need not mean totally doing without much-loved foods. Delicious things, though they shouldn't be eaten in excess, can be saved as treats for special occasions. There are certain foods and flavours for which there is just no substitute – the richness of chocolate, or the texture of a juicy steak – and nothing tastes quite as wonderful as food cooked in butter. Occasional indulgences in these pleasures will not cause harm to our bodies if we feed them on a sensible healthy diet most of the time.

Some of the menus in this book include dishes which are undoubtedly rather rich. These are intended for 'special' meals to be indulged in only on occasion and not as dishes to be eaten daily as part of a normal diet.

The size of the servings in these menus might seem, at first, a little on the small side for some hungry people. I have found most normal appetites to be perfectly satisfied by the amounts of food suggested, but if you are in doubt, add another small, suitable course from another menu, or cook more vegetables, or serve bread with the meal, or perhaps add a cheese or salad course when this would be appropriate. When food is well prepared and beautifully presented, the appetite is much sooner satisfied. A delicious and attractive meal will be savoured slowly and thoughtfully, whereas a mountain of boring food will be devoured quickly with hardly a thought.

DELIGHTING THE EYE

In the presentation of a dish, although appearance is secondary to the quality and taste of the food, one should endeavour to excite the eye as well as the palate. To present a meal which not only gives great pleasure to the stomach but also to the eye is not only satisfying to the cook but is a great compliment to your guests, who are most likely to be your friends. This is what entertaining should be about – giving pleasure to family and friends, and to oneself.

Although it is natural to want to serve as attractive and delicious a meal as possible, it is a great mistake, through over-enthusiasm, to serve food which is either so overwhelmingly different in taste or startling in appearance that it will dominate the evening's conversation.

Fashion in food presentation, like everything else, is subject to change. The elaborately assembled and garnished dishes which impressed our grandparents now appear overdone and amusing to modern tastes. On the other hand, the simple 'country style' of presenting food, popular for so long, is less suited to lighter and more elegant-looking dishes. A new way of serving food, influenced by Japanese taste, and popularized by the fashionable chefs of the *nouvelle cuisine*, provides an exciting and not necessarily complicated alternative.

The most important difference between country style and *nouvelle cuisine* presentation is that food is no longer served at table in dishes from which the diner helps himself, or is served by a waiter. The new way is for small portions of food – of carefully balanced flavours, textures and colours, which the chef or cook decides will create a perfectly harmonious dish – to be attractively and, when appropriate, amusingly arranged on individual plates before being brought to table.

It is not necessary to buy expensive, modern tableware. Hunt in antique fairs and junk shops for linen, glasses, plates and cutlery that will combine well to create the atmosphere to match the food.

This is not as difficult as it might sound and, with careful advance preparation and a little practice, it can add a delightful new dimension to entertaining. Also, it ensures that the table continues to look as attractive right through the meal as it did when guests first sat down. Nothing looks less appealing than a half-carved joint of meat or a partly demolished sweet, no matter how prettily or elaborately presented it was originally.

If a plate of food requires a garnish, this should always be simple and always edible. Also, it should be of a flavour and texture which marries well with and enhances the dish. Parsley, for example, though a delicious and invaluable herb, is greatly overused and should not be sprinkled indiscriminately over all fish dishes, soups, sauces and vegetables. Sometimes it will add the perfect finishing touch to a dish, but at other times its relatively strong taste is too intrusive and will dominate other delicate flavours. A prettily fanned gherkin is another popular garnish. It might add a splash of colour, a touch of sophistication and a welcome sharp note to the flavour of one dish, but could look inappropriate and ruin the flavour of another.

To give a dinner party which is both a pleasant and attractive occasion can only add a little much-needed glamour to our everyday lives. It is fun to create an evening from time to time which is a little less casual than lasagna and salad eaten in jeans and sweatshirts. To create this kind of 'special' occasion certainly requires a little extra time and thought, but it no more needs expensive items to make the table attractive than one needs expensive and unusual ingredients to create delicious food.

Your table setting should reflect the mood of the meal or occasion and be attractive and original without being overpowering. Great impenetrable arrangements of sweet, heavily scented blooms soon overwhelm the taste of delicately flavoured food, and loud background music will quickly inhibit conversation.

China, glass and cutlery need not necessarily be new, or even matching to look elegant. It is fun to hunt for pretty, useful items in jumble and boot sales, antique fairs and junk shops. Everyone loves to find a bargain, but often even the more expensive antique items are, in fact, cheap when compared with the new alternatives. Solid old-fashioned cutlery, though it might perhaps need polishing occasionally, can add so much more style to a table setting than shiny, new inexpensive knives and forks.

Old dinner plates are usually about the same size. A selection of odd plates, collected with a colour theme in mind – perhaps different designs in blue and white – can look charming, and cost very little. Six pretty plates can soon be found to make a set and it is lovely to have several sets to suit a different mood or theme of a meal.

Real damask or linen or lace cloths and napkins, though time-consuming to launder, are so much more attractive and luxurious than easy-care polyester cloths and paper napkins. These can be easily picked up secondhand, and if they will not wash as white as you would like they can look lovely dyed in pretty colours.

Try if possible to think of some simple and original touch to make your table pretty and perhaps seasonal. This does not mean spending a fortune on expensive flowers – in midwinter, a basket of evergreen leaves on a beautifully starched white cloth can look far more stunning than expensive hothouse chrysanthemums. A lace cloth set with delicate pink and white antique china and scattered with the fallen petals of overblown roses will add an extravagantly romantic touch to a candlelit dinner. A single exotic bloom placed by each setting could add just the right, fabulous touch to a tropically inspired meal.

Garden or wild flowers look so much prettier than those from shops which have been cultivated to a uniform colour and size. Tiny individual arrangements of ordinary daisies or a few primroses sitting in eggcups will add a delightful touch of simple country charm to spring dinner parties. As a 'townie' I take great delight in rustic flower arrangements from city weeds such as dandelions and wild grasses.

Just the right quiet music or a delicate perfume of subtle incense, when appropriate, can add just the right finishing touch to a meal with a special mood or theme. When used, these 'special effects' should be simple, discrete and never overpowering. Finally, cooking for the future should not only be light but lighthearted – enjoy it!

SPECIAL EQUIPMENT

Food processors and blenders

There are now many excellent machines of this type on the market. They vary both in price and in the number of jobs they can perform.

Owning one of these machines is as essential to a cook as owning a sharp knife. Even one of the small, cheaper blenders will save endless time and effort in the kitchen. If possible, however, invest in the best food processor you can afford. It will soon become your dearest and most trusted friend in the kitchen, helping you to chop, grate, grind, mince, mix and purée, as well as many other time-consuming and tedious jobs.

Steamers

Steaming is an excellent and healthy way to cook food, particularly vegetables, as none of the nutrients or flavour are leached away by cooking liquids. There are many different types on sale. Lidded metal steamers which fit on top of a saucepan are the most common. Collapsible, perforated metal cages which fit inside different sizes of saucepan are an excellent and cheap alternative (though these are only useful for foods which cook quickly: they do not allow much room underneath in the pan for liquids, and this soon boils away). Most useful is a set of Chinese bamboo steamers which fit one on top of the other, allowing several items to be cooked separately but simultaneously. These steamers can be used in combination with a wok. As the water boils away it is easy to see the level and refill the wok from a kettle. Bamboo steamers are not only inexpensive and efficient, but make a very decorative addition to your kitchen. Available from Chinese and good kitchen supply shops.

Pasta machines

There are two main types of pasta-making machines available in this country. For real addicts of fresh pasta it might be worth buying the expensive type which quickly and effortlessly converts flour and eggs into pasta. These machines are supplied with a selection of

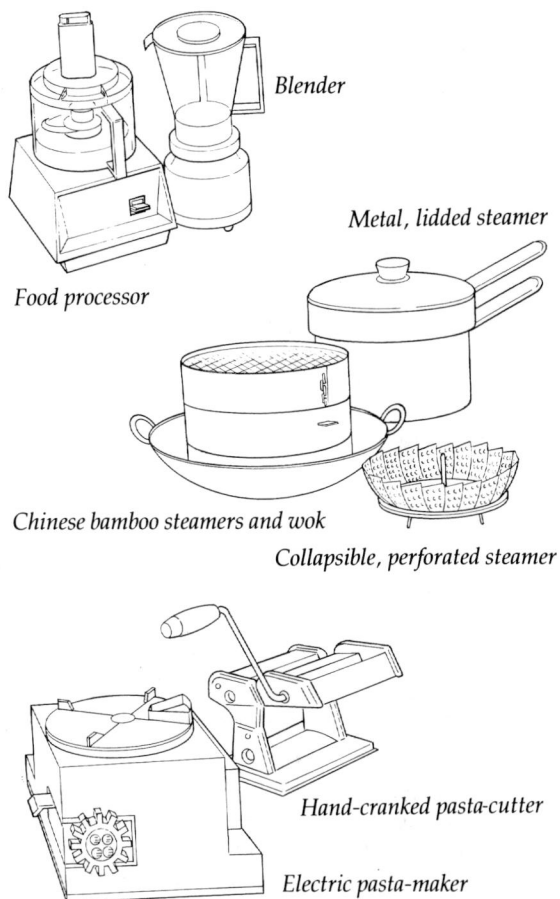

Blender

Food processor

Metal, lidded steamer

Chinese bamboo steamers and wok

Collapsible, perforated steamer

Hand-cranked pasta-cutter

Electric pasta-maker

nozzles which produce the different shapes. A small, metal, hand-cranked machine will efficiently cut dough – made either by hand (see page 18) or in a mixer or food processor – into various shapes – lasagna, tagliatelli, spaghetti, ravioli.

Rice cookers

Most Chinese families own one of these machines, now widely available in this country. They will cook rice to perfection and then keep it hot and in perfect condition for several hours. Available in many sizes, a rice cooker would be a useful addition to the kitchen equipment of those who eat rice frequently. Available from large electrical equipment suppliers and Chinese supermarkets.

BASIC RECIPES

Pasta

270 g/10½ oz flour
3 eggs

Before you begin
Pasta can be made from many kinds of flour,
including wholemeal. Ordinary plain flour is
quite suitable, although strong white bread
flour will give a better result. Italian durum
flour, which has a high gluten content, will
produce pasta with an authentic taste.

1 *Place the flour in the middle of
your work surface and create a well
in the centre. Break in the eggs and
start mixing, drawing in the flour
from the outside of the walls of the
well.*

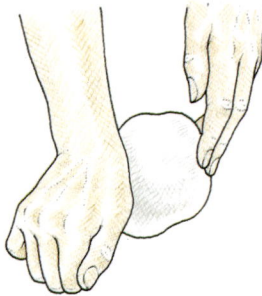

2 *Bring the dough together to form
a solid compact mass, then knead for
10 minutes until smooth.*

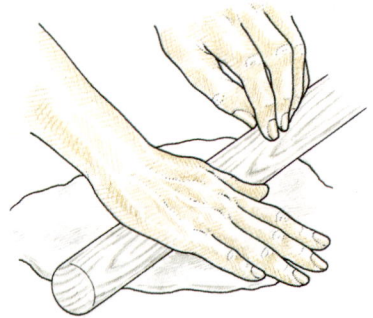

3 *Generously flour a large work
surface. Cut the dough into 4 equal
pieces. Working with one piece at a
time roll out the dough, continually
turning and stretching it until it is
as thin as possible.*

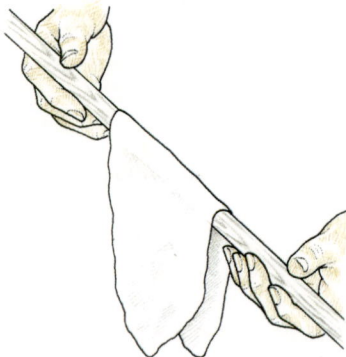

4 *When thin enough to be almost
transparent, hang each sheet of
dough over a pole or broom handle
balanced between the backs of 2
chairs. Leave to dry out for
approximately 45 minutes.*

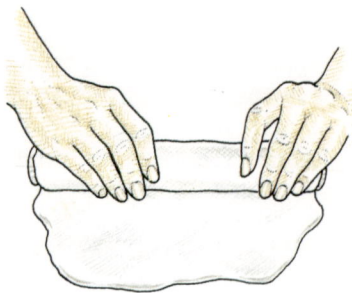

5 *Dust the table with flour and
stack the 4 sheets of dough one on
top of the other, sprinkling flour
between each layer. Roll the layers
together to form a cylinder.*

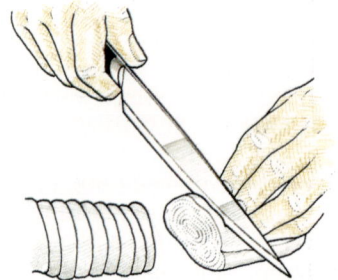

6 *Cut into 1 cm/¼-½ inch slices.
Separate the noodles. Cook in plenty
of boiling salted water for no more
than 3 or 4 minutes. Drain and
serve immediately.*

Basic pale stock no 1 (chicken)

*1 large boiling chicken with giblets,
   weighing approx. 2.25 kg/5 lb,
   cleaned and cut into 8 pieces*
*1 medium onion, washed but with
   the skin left on, quartered*
2 cloves garlic, peeled but left whole
*1 medium carrot, scrubbed and
   roughly chopped*
1 celery stick, chopped (optional)
1 bay leaf
*1 x 5-cm/2-inch strip finely pared
   lemon rind*
10 ml/2 tsp salt
*freshly ground pepper (white, if
   available, is preferable to black as
   it does not leave dark specks in the
   finished stock)*
1.8 litres/3 pints cold water

1 Place all the ingredients in a very large saucepan and slowly bring to the the boil, skimming off any scum as it rises to the surface. Cover the pan tightly and cook over a gentle heat for 2 hours. Alternatively, cook in a slow cooker on low for 8 hours or overnight.
2 Remove the chicken. Take the meat from the bones and discard all skin. Reserve the meat for another use.
3 Strain the stock and discard the solids.
4 Chill the stock for at least 4 hours after it has cooled, preferably overnight, then remove the fat which will have solidified on the surface. The stock is now ready for use.
Note: Other vegetables and herbs can be added to this recipe, but this version uses only those ingredients available all year round. The resulting stock is excellent. It is delicious served on its own as a clear soup, or makes a perfect basis for other soups and sauces. If you want to intensify and concentrate the flavour, reduce the stock, but remember not to add too much salt to the basic stock in the first place as this will also become concentrated on reduction (see page 24). Leaving on the onion skins adds a rich golden colour to the stock.

Basic pale stock no 2 (vegetable)

*100-125 g/4 oz mushrooms, wiped
   and sliced*
*450 g/1 lb onions, washed but skins
   left on, quartered*
*225 g/8 oz carrots, scrubbed and
   roughly chopped*
*225 g/8 oz swede or turnip, peeled
   and roughly chopped*
2 celery sticks, roughly chopped
*½ green or red pepper, cored, seeded
   and roughly chopped*
3 cloves garlic, peeled but left whole
*5-cm/2-inch strip finely pared lemon
   rind*
large bunch of parsley
1 bay leaf
10 ml/2 tsp salt
5 ml/1 tsp sugar
*freshly ground pepper (white, if
   available, is preferable to black as
   it does not leave dark specks in the
   finished stock)*
1.8 litres/3 pints cold water
dash of soy sauce

1 Place all the ingredients in a very large saucepan. Bring to the boil, then cover the pan tightly and simmer gently for 1½ hours.
2 Strain the stock and discard the solids. The stock is now ready for use.
Note: The onion skins add a lively golden glow to the stock. If you want to keep the stock pale, use button mushrooms. Open or field mushrooms will produce a rich dark stock.

Coconut milk

750 ml/1¼ pints boiling water
175 g/6 oz dessicated coconut

Method

1 Pour the boiling water over the coconut in a bowl and leave to soak for 30 minutes.
2 Pour through a wire sieve, collecting the coconut 'milk' in a bowl. Press the coconut solids in the sieve with the back of a wooden spoon to extract as much liquid as possible. Discard the solids.
Note: This recipe should produce about 600 ml/1 pint of coconut milk.

Mayonnaise (blender)

2 whole eggs (at room temperature)
10 ml/2 tsp salt
5 ml/1 tsp dry English mustard
150 ml/¼ pint best olive oil
150 ml/¼ pint tasteless vegetable oil
juice of ½ lemon
freshly ground pepper (white, if
    available, is preferable to black as
    it does not leave dark specks)

1 Place the eggs, salt and mustard in the bowl of a blender or food processor and blend until smooth.
2 With the motor running, add the oils in a very thin steady trickle. You can pour them in a little quicker as the mayonnaise begins to thicken.
3 Add the lemon juice and pepper to taste. Blend for a few more seconds.
4 Check for seasoning: according to taste you might like to add more salt or lemon juice. Now is the time to add other flavourings and herbs, too. If the mayonnaise is too thick, add a little boiling water and blend for 2-3 seconds longer.
Note: This is a very simply made basic mayonnaise which can be varied according to personal taste. Try altering the proportions of the oils, or try vegetable oil with a little nut oil. For a less rich sauce, mix part mayonnaise with part low-fat plain yogurt.

Shortcrust no 1 (rich)

225 g/8 oz plain flour
3.75 ml/¾ tsp salt
110 g/4 oz cold butter, cut into small
    pieces
1 egg yolk, lightly beaten
45 ml/3 tbsp cold water

1 Place the flour and salt in a mixing bowl and rub in the butter until the mixture resembles fine breadcrumbs.
2 Mix in the egg yolk and water and, working quickly, bring together the mixture until it forms a smooth dough.
3 Wrap in plastic wrap and chill for 30 minutes before rolling out.
Note: This dough can be made in a food processor.

Shortcrust no 2 (lard)

225 g/8 oz plain flour
1.25 ml/¼ tsp salt
110 g/4 oz cold lard, cut into small
    pieces
75 ml/5 tbsp cold water

1 Place the flour and salt in a mixing bowl and rub in the lard until the mixture resembles fine breadcrumbs.
2 Mix in the water and, working quickly, bring together the mixture until it forms a smooth dough.
3 Wrap in plastic wrap and chill for 30 minutes before rolling out.
Note: This dough can be made in a food processor.

Suet pastry (basic)

450 g/1 lb self-raising flour
5 ml/1 tsp salt
225 g/8 oz grated or shredded suet

1 Place the flour, salt and suet in a mixing bowl. With a fork stir the mixture, adding just enough cold water to form a firm dough.
2 The pastry does not have to be well mixed. It should be made as quickly as possible and used immediately.
Note: This dough is very versatile and can be used for sweet or savoury dishes. The basic recipe can be varied enormously by adding other flavourings and seasonings, for instance herbs or chopped onions.

Cream cheese pastry

175 g/6 oz plain flour
5 ml/1 tsp caster sugar
2.5 ml/½ tsp salt
75 g/3 oz cold butter, cut into small
  pieces
110 g/4 oz cream cheese, cut into
  small pieces
30-45 ml/2-3 tbsp cold water

1 Place the flour, sugar and salt in a mixing bowl. Rub in the butter and cream cheese until the mixture resembles fine breadcrumbs.
2 Add just enough cold water to the mixture to form a smooth dough. Try 30 ml/2 tbsp at first and add the rest if necessary.
3 Wrap in plastic wrap and chill for at least 30 minutes before rolling out.
Note: This dough can be made in a food processor.

Almond pastry

150 g/5 oz plain flour
75 g/3 oz ground almonds
2.5 ml/½ tsp salt
5 ml/1 tsp caster sugar
125 g/4 oz cold butter, cut into small
  pieces
1 egg yolk, lightly beaten
45 ml/3 tbsp cold water

1 Place the flour, ground almonds, salt and sugar in a mixing bowl. Rub in the butter until the mixture resembles fine breadcrumbs.
2 Mix in the egg yolk and water and working quickly, bring together the mixture until it forms a smooth dough.
3 Wrap in plastic wrap and chill for at least 30 minutes before rolling out.
Note: This dough can be made in a food processor.

Puff pastry

225 g/8 oz plain flour, chilled
2.5 ml/½ tsp salt
225 g/8 oz cold unsalted butter
120 ml/4 fl oz cold water

Before you begin
1 All ingredients should be cold. Keep flour in a refrigerator.
2 Work in as cool an area as possible, on a cold surface. Marble is ideal.
3 Illustrated overleaf is the method up to the first turn. Puff pastry has six turns. After the first turn, repeat the process so that a pair of turns has been made. Cover in plastic wrap and chill for 20 minutes. Then make a second pair of turns. If you intend to keep the dough in the refrigerator for a couple of days or freeze it before use, do so after 4 turns. If frozen, thaw in the refrigerator when required. Complete the final 2 turns and allow to rest once more in the refrigerator before rolling out for baking.
4 To remind you how many turns have been made, at the end of each pair make two (or four) light indentations in the dough.
5 Never allow the egg glaze to dribble down the sides of rolled dough as this will seal the edges and stop the layers from rising properly.

Place the chilled flour and salt in a mixing bowl. Rub in 25 g/1 oz of the butter, then add the water and quickly work with the fingers into a dough. Do not overhandle the dough. Alternatively, this stage can be done in a food processor. Wrap in plastic wrap and chill for 10 minutes.

1 *Lightly flour the remaining cold butter and place it between two sheets of greaseproof paper. With a rolling pin, gently flatten into a 11-cm/4½-inch square. Chill for 10 minutes.*

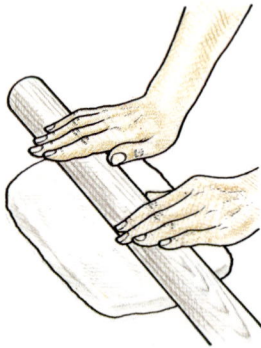

2 *On a floured surface, roll out the dough to a 23-cm/9-inch square shape.*

3 *Remove the paper from the butter and place it diagonally across the centre of the dough.*

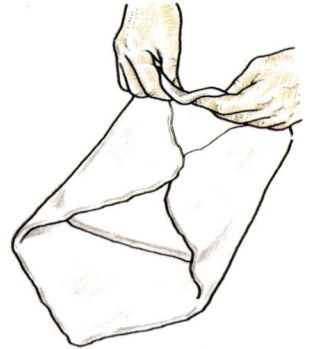

4 *Fold the dough in over the butter square so that it overlaps slightly in the middle like an envelope.*

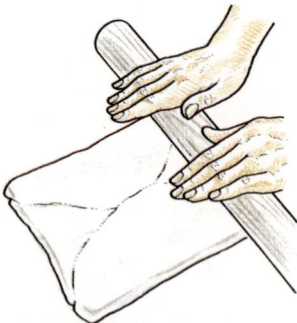

5 *Press lightly with a rolling pin or the fingers to seal the edges and enclose the butter.*

6 *Make the first turn (puff pastry has 6 turns). Turn the pastry parcel seam side down on the floured work surface. Roll out quickly and smoothly into a rectangle which is 2½ times as long as it is wide. Turn the pastry over and, holding the narrow end, fold in thirds.*

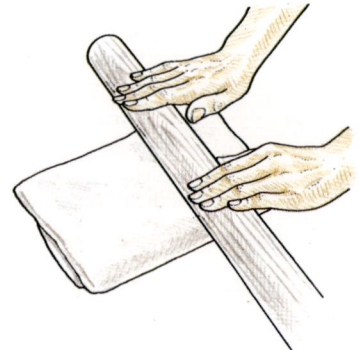

7 *Press down on this gently with the rolling pin to seal the 3 layers.*

BASIC TECHNIQUES

Puff pastry butterflies

This is most successful when using home-made pastry. When making the last 2 turns (see page 21), roll out the dough using granulated sugar instead of flour. Roll out the pastry to a long rectangle, measuring 10 cm/4 inch wide and 1 cm/½ inch thick. Trim the ends and sides of the rectangle, as all the edges should be cut and not folded to allow the pastry to rise and the layers to separate when cooked.

1 Place a rolling pin down the centre of the dough, parallel to the long sides, Then roll and press the edges.

2 Now cut across the rectangle, parallel to the short sides, to make 1 cm/½ inch wide strips.

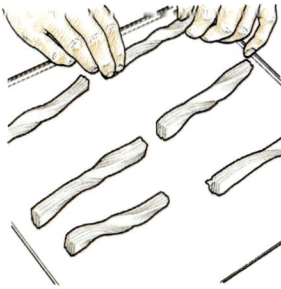

3 Give each strip one twist in the middle, then place them on a dampened, spotlessly clean, baking sheet. Leave plenty of space between each strip to allow room for it to spread and open out into a butterfly shape. Chill for 10 minutes, then bake in a pre-heated 425°F/220°C/Gas 7 oven for approximately 10 minutes or until golden and crisp. Remove while hot to a wire cooling rack and allow to cool completely. If not using immediately, store in an airtight container.

Puff pastry baskets

These can be made successfully with ready-made bought puff pastry. If using home-made, complete the last 2 turns, then roll out the pastry to 1 cm/½ inch thick (fractionally thinner if making the small baskets).

Cut into squares measuring 15 cm/6 inches for the large baskets and 10 cm/4 inches for the small size. Brush the dough squares with beaten egg yolk.

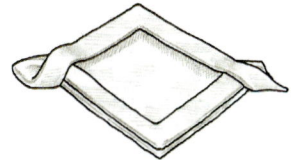

1 Make cuts with a sharp knife, 2 cm/⅝ inch from the edges. In 2 opposite corners, stop the cuts 3 cm/1¼ inches short of the edge.

2 Bring one cut edge over and place along the opposite inside corner of the square. Press down gently with the fingers to seal.

3 Repeat with the opposite corner. Any unglazed areas of the basket should now be brushed with beaten egg yolk. Be careful that none of the glaze runs down the cut edges, as this will seal the layers and stop them from rising properly. Chill for 15-20 minutes. Bake in a preheated 425°F/220°C/Gas 7 oven for approximately 15 minutes or until well risen and golden brown. Remove while hot to a wire rack and allow to cool. If the centre of the basket has risen a lot, cut some of the pastry away and hollow out the centre with a sharp knife. If not to be used immediately, store in an airtight container.

Steaming

Fill the bottom half of the steamer (see page 17) with boiling water and place the food to be cooked in the top perforated half. Sprinkle over a little salt or other seasonings to taste, then cover tightly and steam over a medium heat until cooked.

Vegetables can be placed directly in the top part of the steamer; they should be cut to even sizes. Other foods, such as meat, fish, or dumplings, should be placed on a lightly oiled plate or piece of foil in the top part of the steamer. This not only prevents the cooked food from sticking to the perforated shelf or rack, but also enables the food to be removed more easily. Always keep an eye on the bottom half of the steamer to make sure that the water does not boil dry.

Using gelatine

When using powdered gelatine, always sprinkle the powder over the liquid in which it is to be dissolved. Never add the liquid to the powder or it will form lumps. Leave to soak and swell for 5 minutes, then warm over a gentle heat, stirring constantly until dissolved. Do not allow to boil. Continue as directed in the recipe.

Working with filo pastry

This is a little tricky at first, but practice will soon make matters easy. If the pastry (see page 34) is frozen, thaw it thoroughly, then unroll the dough sheets. Carefully peel away each wafer-thin layer of pastry as required. Work as quickly as possible as the thin sheets soon dry out and then tear or break apart, and keep the rest of the pastry covered with a damp tea-towel all the time you are working. Brush each sheet of pastry with melted butter as it is layered or as instructed in recipe.

Cooking in a bain-marie

A bain-marie is a water bath, a pan of hot water in which a receptacle of cooked food is placed to keep it warm. A bain-marie is also used for cooking – a pan or dish of food (usually a delicate mixture like a custard) is placed in a bath of hot water before it is put in the oven. This ensures an even temperature and more gentle heat all around the cooking vessel. Roasting tins make ideal bain-maries. Place the pan, pot or dish in the roasting tin, then pour in boiling water to come about halfway up the sides of the dish. Place immediately in a pre-heated oven, and cook as the recipe directs.

Reducing liquids

This means to boil a stock, sauce or other liquid over a high heat until some of it evaporates in steam. This 'reduces' the liquid, and concentrates the flavour. Care must be taken not to add too much salt or other seasonings to a liquid which is going to be reduced as these flavours become greatly intensified on reduction.

Cooking pasta

Great care should be taken not to overcook pasta, and to serve it *al dente* – a little firm to the bite – as the Italians do. This particularly applies to fresh pasta, which usually needs approximately 3 minutes cooking time.

Cook the pasta, fresh or dried, in a large pan of rapidly boiling, salted water. Time the cooking from when the water comes back to the boil. Simmer uncovered until done, then quickly drain the pasta and serve immediately. Never rinse pasta, in either hot or cold water, after it is cooked or it will stick together.

An excellent alternative way of cooking dried pasta is to time 3 minutes after the pasta comes to the boil, then tightly cover the pan and remove it from the heat. Leave the pan undisturbed for the cooking time stated on the packet. Now drain the pasta and it will be perfectly cooked.

Gherkin fans

With a small sharp knife make several cuts, as close to each other as possible, down the length of a small gherkin. Leave one end of the gherkin uncut. Open out the slices to produce a fan shape.

Cooking rice

Everyone has their own favourite methods of cooking rice. This is the one I find successful.

Rinse the rice very thoroughly in several changes of water, then place it in a heavy-bottomed saucepan. Add water to the pan to come 2.5 cm/1inch above the level of the rice and salt to taste. Bring the water to the boil and cook over a medium heat until most of the surface liquid has evaporated – 15-20 minutes. Now tightly cover the pan and turn down the heat to as low as possible. Leave the pan undisturbed for 15-20 minutes longer and you will have perfectly cooked, dry, fluffy rice.

Peeling tomatoes

Place the tomatoes in a bowl and pour over enough boiling water to cover. Leave for 1 minute, then remove from the water. Pierce the skin of the tomato with a knife and the skin will slip off easily.

Clarifying butter

Place the butter in a heavy-bottomed saucepan over a very low heat and melt it. Allow the melted butter to simmer very gently for 45 minutes to 1 hour, or until the clarified butter is crystal clear and all the impurities have settled to the bottom of the pan. All the water in the butter will now have evaporated also. Line a sieve with muslin and strain the butter through this into a warm jar or container. Allow to cool and then refrigerate until required.

Julienne strips

A term which refers to cutting vegetables, fruit rind or other foods into narrow strips. These should be about the size of a matchstick, or even smaller and narrower for citrus fruit rind, to be used as a garnish.

Blanching

To blanch any food requires a large pan of rapidly boiling water. Plunge the food into the water and leave for 30 seconds to 2 minutes, depending on the size and type of food. Drain and immediately plunge into very cold water. This stops the food from cooking any further. Drain the food again and pat dry on kitchen paper or clean teatowels. Proceed as directed in the recipe.

Baking blind

Roll out the pastry and use to line the tin which has been buttered and dusted with flour. Trim away the pastry level with the top of the tin. Press a circle of foil into the pastry case to line it and fill with some dried beans or rice to act as weights. Chill for 20-30 minutes. Place in a preheated 425°F/220°C/Gas 7 oven and bake for 10 minutes. Remove from the oven and take out the weights and the foil. Press back gently any bubbles which might have formed in the pastry. Return to the oven and continue to bake until the pastry cases are crisp and golden. The time taken will vary with the type of pastry.

Deglazing

This is a process whereby sediments and juices from cooked foods are mixed into sauces or gravies. The cooked food is removed and the pan in which it was cooked is placed on the heat. Liquid is added to the pan and allowed to simmer while all the bits which are sticking to the bottom of the pan are scraped off and mixed into the liquid. The liquid could be anything – water, stock, vinegar, alcohol, etc. If using alcohol, particularly spirits, these should be flamed – once they have been heated in the pan, they should be set alight. The alcohol will be burnt off, leaving only its flavour and none of the sharpness.

Toasting almonds

Place blanched, split or flaked almonds on a piece of foil under a hot grill. Make sure that they are in an even layer, and watch constantly as they should be toasted only to a pale golden brown. Do not allow them to burn. Once they are golden brown turn the nuts over and toast the other side.

Souring cream

If sour cream is not available, fresh double or whipping cream can successfully be turned into sour cream by adding 5 ml/1 tspn of lemon juice to each 150 ml/¼ pint cream. Stir the lemon juice well into the cream and leave for 30 minutes before use.

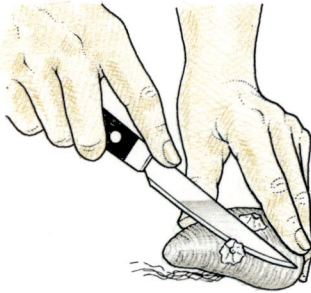

Coping with fresh mussels

1 If the mussels have not already been cleaned you must first scrape away the barnacles from the shells with a sharp knife.

2 Now scrub the shells very thoroughly under cold running water.

3 Next strip away any 'beard' which protrudes from the join in the straight side of the shell and again rinse under cold running water.

4 The mussels should then be soaked in cold water for at least one hour to remove any traces of dirt or sand. Change the water at least three times. Drain the mussels and give any which remain open a sharp tap. Any mussels which remain open are dead and must be thrown away. Also discard those which seem dubious.

5 The mussels are ready to be opened. This is done in a large heavy-bottomed saucepan with a tight-fitting lid. Some recipes will suggest adding wine, shallots or other ingredients at this stage, but unless you are making a soup or are going to serve the mussels in the cooking liquid this is not necessary. Place the mussels in the dry pan, cover it and simply turn on the heat to medium. The pan will not burn because when the mussels open they release quite a lot of their own liquid.

6 Cook for 2-3 minutes, shaking the pan occasionally. Remove the lid and, as the mussels open, take them out of the pan. It is important to take them out as they open because they will become tough and rubbery if allowed to cook for too long. Any that stubbornly refuse to open should be discarded.

7 The mussels are now cooked and ready to eat or to be used for further preparation.

Lining a pudding basin with suet pastry

1 Roll out the dough into a round about 1½ times as wide as the opening of the basin. Cut away one-third of the round in a wedge shape, and reserve this piece for the lid.

2 Pick up the larger segment and form it into a rough cone shape. Ease it into the well-greased basin. Seal the overlapping seam with a little water. Now fill the basin with the contents of the pudding. This should not come higher than two-thirds of the way up the inside of the basin.

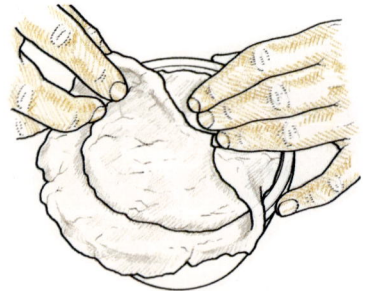

3 Roll out the reserved wedge of dough into a round that will fit just inside the basin. Place this lid over the filling, then bring over the sides of the pastry case, pinching them on onto the lid and sealing with a little water. Tightly cover the basin with foil and steam as directed in the recipe.

Flattening and stuffing a turkey or chicken breast fillet

1 Place a fillet (skinless, boneless breast) on a dampened work surface. Trim away any loose or untidy bits of flesh and reserve for another use. With a dampened rolling pin, carefully beat the meat until it becomes much thinner and larger in area.

2 Now place the fillet stuffing along the centre. The smoother side of the meat should be underneath at this stage.

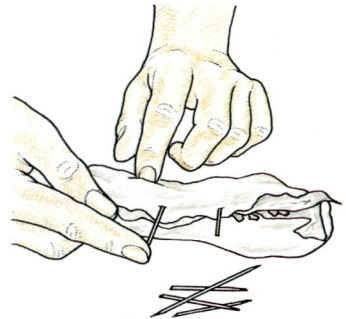

3 Roll the fillet up over the stuffing into a tight cigar shape, tucking in any loose bits and securing the join with wooden cocktail sticks. Cook with the seams underneath as directed in the recipe.

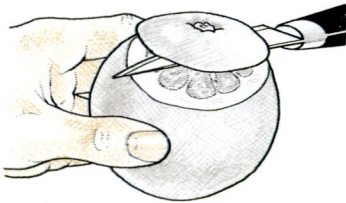

Peeling and segmenting citrus fruits

1, 2 With a sharp knife, peel away the skin from the fruit making sure that you remove all traces of bitter white pith.

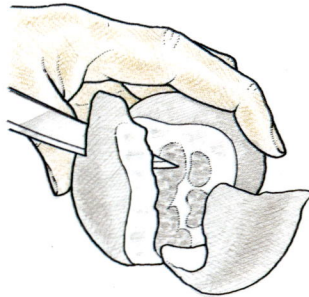

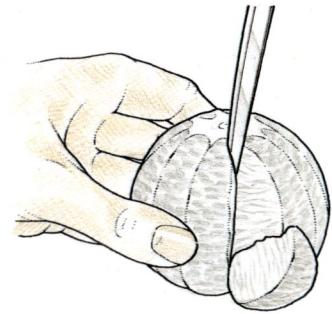

3 Holding the fruit in one hand (over a bowl to catch any juice) cut in between the flesh and close to the membrances that divide the segments, then remove the segments of flesh and leave the unwanted membranes attached to the central core.

Coping with fresh ginger

1 Cut off any small, awkward nobbles and discard.

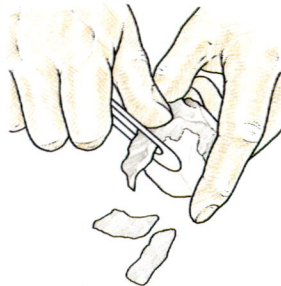

2 Break the remaining piece of root into manageable pieces, and remove the skin with a sharp knife or vegetable peeler.

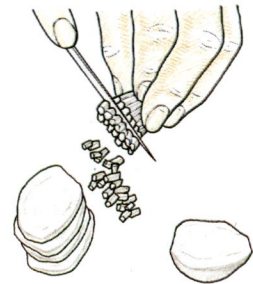

3 Slice or chop the peeled root as required.

INGREDIENTS

HERBS AND SPICES

Fresh herbs always taste better than dried ones. Some herbs, however, do dry well, for example, rosemary, bay and sage. But beware, because the flavour of dried herbs is much more intense than fresh. If a recipe states a measure of fresh herbs, reduce the amount by at least half if using dried ones.

Stale dried herbs will only add an unpleasant musty taste to food, so be sure the dried herbs in your cupboard are not past their best. If in doubt, use another herb or omit herbs completely from a dish. Dried herbs are only suitable in cooked dishes and are most unpleasant when added to raw foods like salads.

Freshly picked herbs can be preserved in other ways for winter use. They can be frozen, or steeped in oils or vinegars.

If at all possible buy spices whole and grind them when needed. Ready-powdered spices have less flavour and do not keep very long. Buy spices in small quantities and store them in a dark place.

Basil (*Ocimum basilicum*)

This delicious sun-loving herb, though not easily found on sale in greengrocers, will grow well in this country in pots on sunny window ledges. It can be preserved in oil or frozen for winter use, but it does not dry well. It is delicious raw, but when used in hot dishes it should only be added towards the end of the cooking time or the flavour will weaken. Its warm, pungent and faintly spicy flavour marries well with most savoury dishes, hot or cold.

Bay (*Laurus nobilis*)

These big shiny evergreen leaves, fresh or dried, are used to flavour food but are never eaten. As their spicy flavour is quite strong, they should be used sparingly – one or even half a leaf is usually sufficient. The flavour of bay blends well with most other flavours and is also used in sweet dishes. A bay leaf is one of the essential ingredients in a bouquet garni.

Chives (*Allium schoenoprasum*)

Easy to grow, these long grass-like leaves with their bright green colour and mild onion taste make an ideal garnish for soups, salads and other dishes. Although delicious in quickly cooked dishes like omelettes, for example, their delicate flavour is soon lost with long cooking.

Coriander (*Coriandrum sativum*)

Very similar in appearance to flat-leaved parsley. Both the leaves and the seeds of coriander are used as flavourings for food. The seeds are strongly aromatic – sweet but with a hint of bitter orange. The leaves combine well with hot and spicy foods, but alone are not to everyones' taste as they have a strong, almost musty flavour.

Oregano (*Origanum vulgare*)

Of the same family and similar in taste to marjoram. The small round green leaves of this herb dry well. A strongly flavoured, versatile herb, oregano blends particularly well with tomatoes and cheese, but is also good in meat, egg and fish dishes.

Parsley (*Petroselinum crispum*)

Our most well-loved and much-used herb. The most familiar variety is the tight curly-leaved type, although Continental or flat-leaved parsley has a better flavour and texture if you can find it.

Rosemary (*Rosmarinus officinalis*)

Most commonly associated with lamb. This pungent herb should be added to food with care, as the flavour can be overpowering. The leaves are hard and spikey, so unless they are chopped very finely, it is better to add this herb to cooking food in sprig form. Remove it before serving. Rosemary dries well.

Thyme (*Thymus vulgaris*)

There are many different varieties of this popular herb, which has a strong, sharp taste. It dries well and its warm pungent flavour blends well with other herbs. It is an essential ingredient in a classic bouquet garni.

Black cumin seeds

The seeds of the wild onion, these are used for their peppery taste. Available from Asian and specialist food shops.

Black mustard seed

These small dark seeds are usually ground to make powdered mustard but can also be used in cooking. Available from Asian and other specialist food shops.

Capers

Used only in their pickled form for their sharp peppery taste, capers are best known as an ingredient in tartare sauce. Easily obtainable.

Caraway seeds

Best known as a flavouring in baking, these long aniseed-flavoured seeds can add an interesting flavour to fish, vegetables and sauces, and taste particularly good with cooked beetroot. Easily obtainable.

Cardamom pods

These seed-filled pods should be slightly crushed before using to release their flavour. With their warm spicy taste they add interest to both sweet and savoury dishes. Widely used in Indian cookery. Easily obtainable.

Chilli powder

Very hot and spicy, this should be added to food with great care as its fieryness can vary greatly. Easily obtainable.

Chinese five-spice powder

This popular Oriental spice consists of equal parts of ground anise pepper, star anise, cinnamon, cloves, and fennel seeds. Its flavour, though subtle, is extremely pungent and should be used with care.

Curry powder

A combination of any number of spices. When bought ready made its flavour can vary enormously according to the recipe used by the particular manufacturer. Although for real curries it is much better to make up your own mixture of spices, a good brand of commercially prepared powder can add a pleasant 'curry' flavour to other dishes if used sparingly. Easily obtainable.

Fennel seeds

These pale long seeds have a slight aniseed taste and can be added to a wide range of dishes, both sweet and savoury. Easily obtainable.

Ginger

A widely used and much loved spice all over the world. In its fresh form and combined with garlic, ginger is one of the essential flavourings in Chinese cookery. In its dried powdered form, it is most commonly used as a flavouring in baking and sweet dishes. Easily obtainable.

Juniper berries

These black, strongly aromatic berries are used dried and whole, although they should be lightly crushed before adding to food so the flavour can be released. Commonly associated with game and other strongly flavoured meats. When used with discretion juniper berries can add an interesting flavour to vegetables and other dishes.

Nutmeg

Always buy this popular spice in its whole form, grating the nut as required. The ready powdered version quickly loses its flavour. Easily obtainable.

Pepper

This should never be bought in powdered form. Always buy whole peppercorns and grind them freshly as required. Black peppercorns are those which are most commonly used. White peppercorns, though more expensive and less easy to find, have a milder taste and when ground into pale soups or sauces do not leave obtrusive little black specks. Easily obtainable.

Sesame seeds

These small whitish seeds are popular as a flavouring in many countries. Best known ground to make tahini paste which flavours Greek humous, they are also popular for decorating cakes and breads. Easily obtainable.

Star anise flower

A popular flavouring in eastern cookery, this aniseed-flavoured spice should be used very sparingly as its flavour, though delicious, can be overpowering. Available from Oriental and specialist food shops.

Turmeric

A basic curry spice. This relative of the ginger family is used in powdered form not only for its spicy taste, but for the vivid yellow colour which it imparts to the food. Easily obtainable.

Whole green peppercorns

These are the unripe seeds of the pepper plant, and have a pleasant mildly peppery and aromatic flavour. They can be bought in small jars or tins, pickled in brine. Available from some delicatessens and specialist food shops.

SEAFOOD

More and more unusual species of fish have started appearing on our fishmongers' slabs over recent years. Don't be afraid to try something new. Many of these 'strange' fish have much better flavours than the familiar cod and haddock, and your own fishmonger will be only too pleased to tell you what they taste like and how to cook them.

Prawns

Uncooked prawns in their shells are not often sold in this country. Buy them if you see them as they are delicious – simply grilled or fried with garlic and butter. Most fishmongers sell ready-cooked prawns in their shells, in varying sizes. Many people find these messy to eat, but a few unshelled prawns can make an attractive garnish for fish dishes. Ready-shelled prawns are usually bought frozen, as, like most shellfish, they quickly deteriorate. Only buy well-known brands, as the cheaper versions are watery and usually completely lacking in flavour. The exception to this is prawns found in the deepfreezes of large Chinese supermarkets. These are generally much less expensive and of excellent quality.

Scallops

Scallops can be bought fresh from the fishmonger when in season – ready-cleaned, uncooked, and usually still attached to one half of the shell. The attractive shells are often used for serving cooked scallops and other fish dishes. Good quality scallops can also be bought frozen. These are normally without shells.

Cockles

These inexpensive and delicious little molluscs are greatly underestimated and have countless culinary possibilities. They are usually sold loose and ready-shelled, in fishmongers and on stalls. Be careful not to buy cockles soaked in vinegar or brine. Cockles can also be bought in jars and tins, but these generally have very little flavour.

Mussels

Fresh mussels are a cheap and delicious treat, and are both quick and simple to prepare (see page 26). They are sold loose or in bags in good fishmongers.

Smoked mussels

These come in small rectangular tins like sardines. Packed in oil, which should be drained away, their strong smokey flavour combines well with other foods and they make a tasty and unusual addition to salads and starters. Available from large supermarkets and delicatessens.

Lumpfish roe

The tiny jet-black fish eggs can be bought quite cheaply in small glass jars. Sometimes called 'poor man's caviar', they are decorative and delicious served in their own right or as a garnish.

Red mullet

Pretty little fish which are becoming more widely available on the fishmongers' slab. Best cooked whole, their delicate sweet-tasting flesh makes a pleasant change from our more everyday fish.

POULTRY AND GAME

Free-range chickens are now becoming more widely available, and though considerably more expensive than fresh or frozen battery chickens, their flavour is far superior. So it is well worth looking for free-range birds and well worth the extra expense.

Boiling chickens (really, old hens) have been rather out of favour for some time, but these 'tough old birds' can have an excellent flavour. After long simmering, the meat is tender and the resulting rich stock can make a wonderful base for soups and sauces. I find them economical and invaluable food.

Chicken and turkey breast fillets

These are now widely available, ready-prepared for cooking, in larger supermarkets. Though quite expensive, they have no skin or fat so there is no waste at all.

Quails

Though very popular and inexpensive on the Continent, these delicious, delicately flavoured little birds are sometimes difficult to find. Buy them when you see them, and, if necessary, freeze them to be used for a special occasion. One bird should be sufficient for each person.

EGGS AND DAIRY PRODUCE

We are advised to cut down on eggs and dairy produce for a healthy modern diet, so let quality rather than quantity be the keynote when buying these ingredients. Buying and eating less, we can afford to buy only the best.

Hens' eggs

Choose free-range eggs whenever possible. Their superior flavour is well worth the extra expense. Available from health food shops and some supermarkets.

Quails' eggs

These tiny eggs taste very little different from hens' eggs. It is their dainty size which makes them a decorative addition to dishes. They are normally served hard-boiled, with or without their pretty spotted shells, and are traditionally accompanied by celery salt. Available from some supermarkets and speciality food shops.

Butter

Unsalted butter is far preferable to salted butter for all purposes. Unsalted butter is more expensive, but it is far better to cut down on your total butter intake and enjoy the wonderful flavour that small amounts of really good fresh butter give to cooked food.

Clarified butter

This is butter which, by a process of heating and straining, has had all its impurities removed (see page 25). This enables it to be heated to a higher temperature than normal butter without burning. It also has the added advantage of being attractively transparent. Known as *ghee*, it is widely used in Indian cookery.

Mozzarella cheese

An Italian curd cheese, mozzarella was originally made from buffalo's milk, but is now made exclusively from cow's milk. It is sold in many forms, the best being that in small paper packets kept fresh in cold water. It is often teamed with tomatoes and used raw in salads, as well as being used in cooked dishes. The mild flavour, creamy texture and excellent melting qualities make this a perfect cheese for pizzas, lasagne and toasted sandwiches.

Parmesan cheese

One of the world's most expensive cheeses. Italy's most famous, genuine Parmesan can be easily recognized by the distinctive dotted lettering in which the name Parmesan is printed on the hard rind. Always buy Parmesan in the piece and grate it at the last minute. It will keep fresher if stored in the freezer and can be grated from frozen. Never buy the ready-grated kind sold in little drums because this is always dry and stale and has an unpleasant acrid taste. If you have no fresh Parmesan, do without or substitute another fresh cheese rather than resorting to the ready-grated type. Available from large supermarkets, Italian delicatessens and specialist food shops.

Goats' cheese

This is sold in many forms and comes from many different countries, but it usually has a pleasant sourish but mild taste. Health food shops often sell small home-made fresh goats' cheeses made by local producers. Look out for them as they are usually excellent.

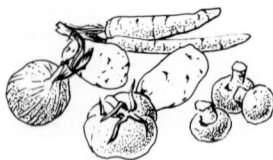

VEGETABLES

Because of the Common Market and advanced modern transportation systems greengrocers – even in small towns – are able to stock an extraordinarily wide variety of fruits and vegetables all the year round. Now we need no longer get bored with any particular vegetable as it comes near to the end of its season, or resort to tinned and processed vegetables in winter to relieve the monotony of carrots, sprouts and cabbage. The first home-grown vegetables in season will, of course, always be a treat, but how wonderful it is to supplement them with a wide variety of other fresh vegetables from all over the world.

Asparagus

Although frozen or even tinned asparagus can be used quite successfully in soups or sauces, only fresh asparagus should be served as a vegetable. When out of season substitute another fresh vegetable.

Bean sprouts

Although most grains, large seeds and beans can be sprouted, the most frequently available commercially are sprouted mung beans. Bean sprouts are a popular feature in Chinese cookery, where they are always cooked, but raw they make a delicious and nutritious salad ingredient. Now widely available.

Broad beans

Luckily this delicious vegetable freezes quite well as the season for fresh broad beans is so short. When in season fresh small broad beans are delicious raw in salads.

Chicory

A long, greenish-white, torpedo-shaped vegetable. The tightly packed leaves add a pleasant bitter taste to salads. Chicory can also be cooked to be served hot, usually slowly braised in the oven with lemon juice, sugar and butter.

Chinese straw mushrooms

These tasty litle mushrooms, which are dark in colour and almost round, are found in tins in this country. Available from large supermarkets, Chinese grocers and specialist food shops.

Dandelion leaves

Popular on the Continent, dandelion leaves are grown commercially for sale in greengrocers there, particularly in France. A few small leaves add a refreshingly bitter note to salads. Only small young leaves should be eaten. Found everywhere!

Dried mushrooms

Buy either the Chinese or the Italian variety. Although they are quite expensive, a little goes a long way, and they swell considerably when soaked. A few added to a dish containing ordinary mushrooms brings out the flavour extremely well. Available from Chinese grocers, Italian delicatessens and specialist food shops.

Fennel

Hard roundish white bulbs with feathery bright green leaves. The green leaves are usually removed, but can be used as a herb as well as a garnish for fish dishes. The bulbs pull apart into thick white 'leaves' which have a crisp celery-like texture and an interesting aniseed taste. Fennel is used raw in salads, but it is also good cooked. In Italy, fennel is often served at the end of a meal as we might serve celery here.

Nettles

When cooked, nettles have a flavour rather like spinach but slightly sweeter. They are good as a vegetable on their own or used in soups and sauces. Only the small leaves from the top of fresh young plants should be used; the older leaves have an unpleasant bitter taste. Wear rubber gloves for picking. Available all too easily.

Okra

Also known as ladies' fingers, okra is a common ingredient in African and Asian cookery. The pointed, ridged green pods can be used in soups and stews or as a vegetable on their own. Available from Asian and West Indian shops and some specialist food shops.

Palm hearts

A tropical delicacy. The tender shoots of some varieties of palm trees, these are sold pre-cooked in tins. Palm hearts are usually served cold as part of a salad or starter. Available from delicatessens and specialist food shops.

Primrose flowers and leaves

These are added to salads as a decorative 'conceit' rather than for their flavour although the leaves do have a pleasant slightly peppery taste. Only pick wild primroses (very few) if they are growing in great numbers.

Pumpkin

This is a much underrated and under-used vegetable in this country. Best known as the basis for American pumpkin pie, the flesh of this inexpensive vegetable has a gorgeous golden colour and a delicious mild sweet flavour. It is good in soups and sauces but excellent when served simply as a vegetable. Combines well with salty or smoked foods.

Spinach

Though it is always preferable to use a vegetable in its fresh form this is one of the few vegetables which freezes very well.

Sweet potato

This sweet orange-fleshed root can be cooked like other potatoes. If unobtainable parsnips would make an adequate alternative. Now generally widely available.

Truffles

These extraordinary small black funghi are rightly known as 'black gold' because they must be the most expensive foodstuff in the world. Rarely seen fresh in this country, they can occasionally be found on sale in tiny tins. If allowed to 'star' in a meal rather than being used merely as an extravagant garnish for other expensive luxury foods like foie gras and lobster, their high cost becomes more realistic. The pasta recipe with truffles in this book, for example, will feed six people for rather less than a traditional roast beef dinner (see page 61). Available from some delicatessen and specialist food shops.

Water chestnuts

These crunchy little round white 'nuts' are widely used in Chinese cooking, where they are always eaten cooked (the Chinese never eat uncooked foods of any sort). They are, however, excellent raw and good in salads. Found ready-to-eat in tins in large supermarkets, Chinese shops, delicatessens and specialist food shops, and occasionally fresh in Chinese grocers.

PASTRY, PASTA, BREAD AND RICE

Filo pastry

These paper-thin sheets of pastry are much used in Greek and Middle Eastern cookery. It is bought ready-made, usually frozen, and can be made into sweet or savoury dishes. It must be used up quickly once opened (see page 24). Available from large supermarkets, Greek grocers and specialist food shops.

Puff pastry

Excellent frozen, ready-made puff pastry is widely available, but if you have never made your own, try it, if only just once. You will be surprised at the difference in flavour and texture. The pleasure which making puff pastry gives is rather like that warm comfortable feeling one gets from making bread (see pages 21 and 22).

Fresh pasta

Luckily, more and more grocers shops are beginning to sell fresh pasta. Buying ready-made fresh pasta provides the basis for a quickly cooked, delicious and inexpensive meal. Making your own, by hand, can be a very pleasurable and rewarding occupation, and anyone who has ever made bread or pastry will find it very easy. There are also various machines on the market to make the job easier (see page 17).

Dried pasta

Available in a wide variety of shapes and sizes, dried pasta is an extremely valuable and nutritious food. Always make sure that the pasta you buy is made from hard 'durum' wheat flour.

Chinese egg noodles

These are available in dried blocks, wrapped in cellophane. The noodles are cooked very quickly in boiling water and can also be fried afterwards. Widely available in big supermarkets, delicatessens and specialist food shops. Chinese grocers sometimes sell fresh noodles, which are excellent.

Bread

Always buy good bread. Wholemeal and granary bread, for example, not only are far more nutritious than white bread but taste so much better and do not need smothering with fattening butter and spreads to be palatable. Once converted to this sort of bread even 'real' crusty French loaves begin to seem tasteless and flabby.

Pitta bread

These flat Greek breads are commonly associated with their popular 'takeaway' filling of kebab and salad. Now widely available either white or wholemeal. I much prefer the brown variety, but it can look most attractive to serve both types.

Fast-action yeast

Many cooks swear by the superior results from baking with fresh yeast, but this is not always easy to buy. I find the new 'fast-action' dried yeast, which is added to the dry ingredients in a recipe and only requires one rising, most efficient and well suited to my busy lifestyle. I have used it throughout this book, wherever yeast is called for.

Basmati rice

The most flavoursome of long-grain rices and much used in Indian cookery. Widely available.

Arborio rice

A round Italian rice used specifically in risottos for its liquid-absorbing qualities. When cooked, the outside of the grains become soft and creamy while the centre remains a little firm to the bite. Available from large supermarkets, Italian delicatessens and specialist food shops.

SAUCES, FLAVOURINGS, CONDIMENTS AND OILS

Soy sauce

This best-known of Oriental condiments is invaluable in the Western kitchen as a versatile seasoning. There are two types, light and dark. The light sauce has a milder flavour but is saltier, and is ideal for cooking. Dark soy sauce is almost black and much thicker, making it perfect for use as a dipping sauce. Dark soy sauce is easily obtainable. Light soy sauce is available from Oriental grocers and specialist food shops.

Hoisin sauce

This thick, dark, reddish-brown sauce is sometimes called barbecue sauce. As its name implies its sweet spicy flavour is ideal with roasted or barbecued meat and other strong-flavoured foods. It is available in large supermarkets, Chinese grocers and delicatessens.

Chinese plum sauce

Lighter in colour and fruitier tasting than hoisin sauce, Chinese plum sauce adapts well to Western dishes and is particularly delicious with cold meats. It is available in large supermarkets, Chinese grocers, and delicatessens.

Sweet chilli sauce

This is thicker and less fiery than normal chilli sauce, and as the name implies has a sweet taste. It is used in Oriental cookery mostly as a dipping sauce. Available from large supermarkets, Chinese grocers and delicatessens.

Horseradish sauce or relish

It is difficult to find fresh horseradish to make your own sauce, but the ready-made versions sold in jars are very good. Though traditionally associated with roast beef, the hot pungent taste of horseradish is also good with smoked fish, and it can give an unusual piquant note to sauces. It makes an interesting alternative to mustard.

Mayonnaise

There are now many excellent varieties of ready-made 'real mayonnaise' on sale which are quite adequate if time is scarce. However, with the help of modern blenders and food processors, it is incredibly simple and quick to make your own mayonnaise. It is also much cheaper (see page 20).

Preserved stem ginger

These round nuggets of fresh ginger preserved in thick sugar syrup are sold in glass jars and are quite expensive to buy. Their hot sweetness can add a deliciously different touch to both sweet and savoury dishes. Available from large supermarkets and delicatessens.

Pickled walnuts

These are one of the few foods which are jet black, and their colour combined with their sharp interesting flavour makes them an attractive and interesting garnish. Use them with discretion as their strong taste would overpower delicately flavoured dishes. Pickled walnuts can be bought, in glass jars, from large supermarkets and delicatessens.

Olive oil

Only buy olive oil which has the words 'extra virgin' printed on the label. It is better to use a flavourless vegetable oil than spoil the flavour of food by using cheap olive oil. Those who profess not to like the taste of olive oil have probably only ever tasted the inferior kind.

Vegetable oils

The oil which is highest in polyunsaturated fat and has the least flavour is safflower oil. Second best are cornflower, corn and soyabean oils. Avoid cheaper oils which are just labelled 'vegetable oil' as these are often a mixture of oils – usually including those high in saturated fat – and give an unpleasant 'oily' flavour to foods cooked in them.

Nut and other oils

The most widely available of these luxury oils is walnut, and hazelnut can also be obtained. Because they are strong in flavour they should be used sparingly. Sesame oil is used in Oriental cookery, and it has an interesting burnt, nutty flavour. Again it needs to be used sparingly and it is particularly good as an addition to salad dressing. Available from large supermarkets and delicatessens.

FRUIT

More and more tropical and unusual fruit is appearing on the shelves of greengrocers and supermarkets in this country. The ones used in this book – mango, papaya, guava, watermelon, kiwi fruit and figs – are just the tip of the iceberg. Don't be afraid to experiment and try some of these strange new flavours. They are often relatively expensive, but a little, when added to more familiar and cheaper fruit, will add a touch of exotic glamour.

MISCELLANEOUS

Arrowroot

This nutritious starch is the powdered extract of the roots of various tropical plants. It is useful as a thickening agent as it is tasteless and a liquid thickened with arrowroot will remain attractively transparent. Widely available from chemists and grocers.

Black pudding

A delicious sausage made from pigs' blood with groats, fat, oatmeal and seasonings. It is similar to the French *boudin noir*. The thought of eating black pudding is not attractive to some people whereas others adore it. Do not serve it to your guests without first finding out which of these two categories they belong to.

Chestnut purée

To make chestnut purée by hand from fresh chestnuts is a very time-consuming business. I have, therefore, in this book used tinned chestnut purée. This is available either sweetened (when it is usually called chestnut spread) or unsweetened, from large supermarkets and delicatessens.

Gelatine

This is available either in its powdered form or as thin transparent sheets. I have used the powdered form throughout this book as it is much more readily available.

Suet

Suet is the hard fat found around beef kidneys. This can be bought in the piece from a butcher and grated at home, or ready shredded in cardboard packs from a grocers or supermarket. Suet gives a delicious and particular flavour to pastries and puddings, but should only be used occasionally and in moderation as it is high in saturated fats.

Tofu

Tofu or beancurd is made from soyabean milk in a process similar to that of making cheese. The resulting curd is available in many forms and is popular in cookery throughout the East because it is an invaluable and inexpensive form of very low-fat protein. The smooth texture of tofu acts as a foil for other foods and quickly absorbs other flavours, having very little taste of its own.

There are two types of tofu available widely in this country. The first is bought as firm white cubes, rather similar in appearance to Greek feta cheese. This is ideal for frying. The second type is 'long-life' and is sold in small cardboard cartons. Known as silken tofu, this will keep indefinitely unopened. Silken tofu has a smooth, thick, junkety texture. It is unsuitable for frying, but perfect for making creamy sauces, dips, dressings and desserts. Tofu is available from Chinese grocers and good health food shops.

THE RECIPES

The recipes that follow have been arranged in dinner party menus, which have been compiled with all the important elements of health, freshness, taste and balance in mind. But this does not mean that the dishes should not be cooked individually, or swapped around from one menu to another. Indeed, some individual recipes, it is hoped, will become part of the regular cook's repertoire and some of the ideas will be assimilated and reappear in new dishes. All recipes will serve six people.

WINTER FRESHNESS

Midwinter, and the countryside is silent and sleeping. Spring seems a very long way off. There is very little now to tempt us out of doors, but we can cheer ourselves through the long, dark evenings by cooking delicious meals and sharing them with friends.

On land, the cold damp earth is still, but the seas and oceans are alive with myriads of species of fish and shellfish. Our fishmongers' slabs are at their most varied, displaying an excellent selection. Many less familiar but delicious varieties come to us from warmer waters. After all the rich and hearty meals of the festive period, this wealth of fresh fish provides a deliciously light and varied alternative.

We need not restrict our diets to a few locally grown and monotonous winter vegetables, but can include some of the marvellous selection of imported foreign produce.

Little mushroom puddings

●

Sautéed seafood with ginger and lime

●

Grape jellies with citrus fruits

Little mushroom puddings

15 ml/1 tbsp olive oil
1 medium onion, peeled and
  chopped
225 g/8 oz fresh mushrooms, sliced
15 g/½ oz dried Chinese or Italian
  mushrooms, soaked for 1 hour in
  warm water, drained and chopped
1 clove garlic, peeled and crushed
1 small truffle, fresh or tinned,
  finely chopped (optional)
pinch of fresh thyme (or dried if not
  available)

salt and pepper
120 ml/4 fl oz red wine
6 gherkin fans (see page 24)

The pastry
450 g/1 lb self-raising flour
225 g/8 oz shredded suet
½ small red pepper, cored, seeded
  and finely chopped
salt and pepper
250 ml/8 fl oz water

1 Heat the oil in a saucepan and cook the onion until transparent. Add all the mushrooms, the garlic, the truffle (if used) and the thyme and season generously with salt and pepper. Cook, covered, over a low heat for 15 minutes, stirring occasionally. Remove from the heat and allow to cool.

2 Make the suet pastry: mix the flour, suet and red pepper in a bowl and season with salt and pepper. Add the water and mix with a fork to form a dough. Gather together with floured hands and, on a floured surface, form into a rough sausage shape. Divide this into 6 equal portions.

3 Roll out each portion of dough to a rough circle about 5 mm/¼ inch thick (see page 26). Cut one-third of each circle away in a wedge shape, and reserve.

4 Grease 6 individual pudding bowls and, using the larger segments of the pastry, carefully line the bowls, pushing the dough well into the corners. Divide the mushroom filling between the bowls but do not allow the filling to come more than two-thirds of the way up the bowls. Pour the wine over the filling just to cover.

5 Cut circles from the remaining segments of pastry to fit just inside the bowls. Place these over the filling and bring over the pastry 'walls', pinching them onto the lids to seal. There should still be a space at the top of the bowls to allow the puddings to rise. Cover each bowl tightly with a small circle of greased foil.

6 Steam over boiling water for 1½ hours.

7 To serve, turn the puddings out onto 6 heated plates and garnish with the gherkin fans.

Sautéed seafood with ginger and lime

50 g/2 oz butter
2 leeks, trimmed and sliced
* crossways*
700 g/1½ lb assorted firm fish,
* such as salmon and cod, filleted*
* and cubed*
2 cloves garlic, peeled and
* crushed*
2.5 cm/1 inch cube of root ginger,
* peeled and finely chopped*

350 ml/12 fl oz green ginger wine
10 ml/2 tsp arrowroot
juice of 2 small limes (or lemons if
* not available)*
salt and pepper
225 g/8 oz peeled, cooked prawns,
* thawed if frozen*

1 Melt the butter in a frying pan and gently sauté the leeks, being careful not to let the butter brown. When the leeks are soft, transfer to a bowl with a slotted spoon and keep warm.
2 Sauté the fish in the same pan very gently until no longer transparent-looking. Do not overcook. Remove with a slotted spoon and put with the leeks to keep warm.
3 Add the garlic and ginger to the pan and fry for 2 minutes. Add the ginger wine and let this bubble for 2 minutes, stirring in all the bits from the bottom of the pan. Mix the arrowroot with the lime juice and add this to the pan to thicken the sauce. Season to taste with salt and pepper.
4 Just before serving, add the prawns to the sauce and stir gently over the heat for a few seconds until they are just warm. Do not overcook or the prawns will become tough.
5 To serve, spoon the fish and leeks onto 6 hot plates and pour over the prawns and ginger sauce.

Grape jellies with citrus fruits

1 sachet powdered gelatine
600 ml/1 pint white grape juice
* (bottled or from a carton)*
a little Cointreau or other
* orange-flavoured liqueur*
* (optional)*

3 oranges, peeled and divided into
* segments (see page 27)*
3 grapefruits, peeled and divided
* into segments (see page 27)*

1 Dissolve the gelatine in a little of the grape juice according to the instructions on the packet. Add to the rest of the juice and stir well. Pour into 6 dampened individual moulds. Leave in the refrigerator until completely set.
2 Meanwhile, if using the liqueur, combine it with the orange and grapefruit segments and leave to macerate for 30 minutes.
3 To serve, quickly dip the moulds individually in hot water, then turn out the jellies onto 6 chilled plates. Arrange alternate orange and grapefruit segments around each jelly and pour over the liqueur. Serve immediately.

Left: Little mushroom puddings
Above: Sautéed seafood with ginger and lime
Below: Grape jellies with citrus fruit

Mussels stuffed with curried garlic and Parmesan

●

Scallops in chicory sauce with steamed cucumber

●

Pears three ways

Mussels stuffed with curried garlic and Parmesan

75 g/3 oz grated Parmesan cheese
½ tbsp/30 ml chopped parsley
60 ml/4 tbsp fresh wholemeal
    breadcrumbs
50 g/2 oz softened butter
2 cloves garlic, peeled and crushed
5 ml/1 tsp curry powder
salt and pepper
90-100 mussels on the half shell
    (see page 26)

1 Mix the Parmesan, parsley, breadcrumbs, butter, garlic and curry powder together and season generously with salt and pepper. Use this mixture to 'stuff' the mussels, spooning a little onto each mussel in its shell.

2 Arrange the mussels in one layer on a baking sheet. Place in a 450°F/230°C/Gas 8 oven and cook only until the butter in the stuffing has melted and the mussels feel hot to the touch. This will take 10-15 minutes. Do not overcook as the mussels will soon become tough.

3 To serve, divide between 6 plates and serve immediately. These are ideal to hand round at a drinks party.

Scallops in chicory sauce with steamed cucumber

450-700 g/1-1½ lb scallops
75 g/3 oz butter
1 cucumber, cut into small sticks
salt

The sauce
50 g/2 oz butter
20 ml/1 heaped tbsp finely
    chopped onion
150 g/5 oz chopped chicory leaves
10 ml/2 tsp sugar
salt and pepper
60 ml/4 tbsp white wine
juice of ½ lemon
300 ml/½ pint single cream

1 First, make the sauce. Melt the butter in a saucepan and cook the onion over a low heat for a few minutes until transparent. Add the chicory, the sugar and a generous seasoning of salt and pepper. Cook, covered, for 15 minutes shaking the pan occasionally.

2 Add the wine and turn up the heat. Cook uncovered until all the wine has evaporated. Add the lemon juice and cream and continue to cook over a medium heat, uncovered, for 10 minutes.

3 Meanwhile, fry the scallops in the butter over a gentle heat, turning once only until they are hot and no longer transparent. Do not overcook as they soon become tough.

4 At the same time, steam the cucumber, sprinkled with a little salt, over boiling water until hot, 5-10 minutes.

5 To serve, divide the scallops between 6 heated plates, spoon over the sauce and add the cucumber.

Pears three ways

6 large ripe pears
juice of 1½ lemons
30 ml/2 tbsp caster sugar
1 egg white, whisked until stiff
    but not dry
2 cardamom pods, crushed
juice of 1 orange
30 ml/2 tbsp water

1 Cut 3 of the pears in half and discard the cores. Scoop out the flesh, leaving the skins unbroken to make containers for the sorbet. Brush the inside of the skins with the juice of ½ lemon to prevent discoloration. Place immediately in the freezer and leave to chill.

2 Blend the pear flesh in a liquidizer or food processor with half of the sugar until completely smooth. Press through a wire sieve into a shallow container and freeze until 'slushy'.

3 Mix well with a fork to break down the ice crystals, and fold in the whisked egg white. Return to the freezer and leave until almost firm. Mix well again with a fork, and pile into the now frozen pear skins. Return to the

freezer until 1 hour before required, then keep in the refrigerator.

4 Meanwhile, peel the remaining 3 pears. Cut them in half and remove the cores. Neatly slice 3 of the halves and toss in the remaining lemon juice. Chill.

5 Chop the remaining pear halves and place in a small saucepan with the remaining sugar, the cardamom, orange juice and water. Cook, covered, over a low heat for 15 minutes. Discard the cardamom and liquidize, sieve and chill.

6 To serve, place 1 sorbet-filled pear half on each of 6 chilled plates. Arrange some of the pear slices in a fan shape next to this and pour over the sauce. Serve immediately.

Above: Mussels stuffed with curried garlic and Parmesan
Right: Scallops in chicory sauce with steamed cucumber
Left: Pears three ways

Fennel-scented leek soup with shellfish

•

Fillets of smoked mackerel in filo pastry with creamed horseradish sauce

•

Lemon sauce pudding

Fennel-scented leek soup with shellfish

50 g/2 oz butter
1 rasher smoked, streaky bacon, rinded and cut into small pieces
450 g/1 lb leeks, trimmed and sliced crossways
225 g/8 oz potatoes, peeled and chopped
salt and pepper
1.25 ml/¼ tsp fennel seeds
900 ml/1½ pints chicken stock (see page 19)
600 ml/1 pint milk
100-125 g/4 oz cockles, cooked and shelled (see page 30)
100-125 g/4 oz peeled cooked prawns, thawed if frozen
6 small circles of toasted white bread

1 Melt the butter in a large saucepan and cook the bacon over a low heat until the fat begins to run from the bacon. Add the leeks and potatoes. Season with salt and pepper and add the fennel seeds. Cook for 5 minutes, stirring constantly. Add the stock and milk, cover the pan and simmer over a low heat for 20 minutes.
2 Liquidize the soup and return to the saucepan. Add the cockles and prawns, keeping back a few for garnish. Simmer for 2 minutes only – any longer and the shellfish will toughen.
3 Arrange one or two reserved prawns and cockles on each toast circle.
4 To serve, divide the soup between 6 heated bowls or soup plates and float one of the shellfish-topped toast circles on each.

Fillets of smoked mackerel in filo pastry with creamed horseradish sauce

3 fillets smoked mackerel, each
weighing about 175 g/6 oz,
skinned and halved lengthways
6 sheets filo pastry (see page 34)
50 g/2 oz butter, melted
75 g/3 oz softened cream cheese

pepper
juice of ½ lemon
300 ml/½ pint single cream
30 ml/2 tbsp horseradish sauce or
relish (in a jar)
freshly cooked seasonal vegetable

1 Brush each sheet of filo pastry with melted butter and fold it over in half. Lay a piece of fish on one edge of each pastry rectangle. Spread the cream cheese over the fish and sprinkle with pepper and lemon juice. Fold over the edges of the pastry and roll up to make a neat long rectangular package. Arrange these on a buttered baking sheet, with the seams underneath.
2 Brush each parcel with melted butter and bake in a preheated 230°C/450°F/Gas 8 oven for 8-10 minutes or until the pastry is crisp and golden.
3 Meanwhile, heat the cream with the horseradish sauce or relish in a small saucepan and season to taste with salt and pepper.
4 To serve, place one of the 'parcels' on each of 6 hot plates. Spoon the vegetable on one side and the sauce to the other.

Lemon sauce pudding

150 g/5 oz butter
250 g/9 oz caster sugar
5 eggs, separated
70 g/2½ oz plain flour
grated rind and juice of
2½ lemons
good 325 ml/½ pint milk

1 Cream the butter and sugar together until pale. Beat in the egg yolks, then stir in the flour and the lemon rind and juice. Stir in the milk. The mixture may look a little curdled at this stage.
2 Whisk the egg whites until stiff but not dry. Fold into the lemon mixture.
3 Pour into a well-buttered, shallow 1.8-litre/3-pint ovenproof dish. Bake in a bain-marie (see page 24) in a preheated 180°C/350°F/Gas 4 oven for 35-40 minutes or until the sponge topping is golden brown and feels firm in the middle. Underneath, however, the mixture will have separated to form a slightly runny sauce.
4 To serve, spoon into 6 bowls or plates. This is best served straight from the oven, but is also good served cold.

Above: Fennel-scented leek soup with shellfish
Left: Lemon sauce pudding

Above: Fillets of smoked mackerel in filo pastry with creamed horseradish sauce

Terrine of smoked fish with whisky prawn sauce
•
Lambs' kidneys with port in puff pastry baskets
•
Watercress, orange and fennel salad

Terrine of smoked fish with whisky prawn sauce

450 g/1 lb smoked cod or haddock
    fillets, skinned
1.25 ml/¼ tsp fennel seed
4 egg whites
300 ml/½ pint single cream
salt and pepper
lumpfish roe (optional)
6 lemon slices, cut into triangles

The sauce
30 ml/2 tbsp whisky
4 egg yolks
300 ml/½ pint single cream
salt and pepper
50 g/2 oz shelled cooked prawns,
    thawed if frozen, roughly chopped

1 Put the fish, fennel seeds, eggs whites and cream into the container of a blender or food processor and blend until perfectly smooth. Generously season with salt and pepper and blend in. Pour the fish mixture into a very generously buttered 900-ml/1½-pint loaf tin or mould.

2 Bake in a bain-marie (see page 24) in a pre-heated 180°C/350°F/Gas 4 oven for 35-40 minutes or until completely set.

3 Meanwhile, make the sauce. Heat the whisky in a small saucepan and flambé to burn off the alcohol. Allow to cool, then place in the container of the blender or food processor with the egg yolks and blend until smooth. Heat the cream in a small pan to almost boiling, then pour in a steady stream onto the mixture in the blender with the motor running. Season to taste with salt and pepper.

4 Pour the sauce into a bowl set in a pan of gently simmering water, or into a double boiler. Stir constantly until it reaches a pouring consistency. Check the seasoning and stir in the prawns.

5 To serve hot, turn out the terrine onto a plate or board and slice. Place one slice on the centre of each plate and surround with the sauce. Decorate with a little lumpfish roe if desired and a tiny triangle of lemon.

6 To serve cold, allow the terrine to cool in the mould before turning out. Allow the sauce to cool before serving.

Note: Should the sauce separate, return to the blender for a few seconds to reblend it.

Lambs' kidneys with port in puff pastry baskets

12 lambs' kidneys
6 large puff pastry baskets (see
page 23)
50 g/2 oz butter
30 ml/2 tbsp chopped onion
300 ml/½ pint chicken or
vegetable stock (see page 19)

45 ml/3 tbsp port
generous 5 ml/1 tsp dry English
mustard
15 ml/1 tbsp redcurrant jelly
salt and pepper
45 ml/3 tbsp single cream
freshly cooked seasonal vegetables

1 Pour enough boiling water over the kidneys to cover and leave to soak for 2 minutes. Drain. Remove the skins and cut into bite-sized pieces, removing the hard core and any large tubes.
2 If the pastry baskets have been prepared in advance, reheat them in the oven while cooking the kidneys.
3 Melt the butter in a frying pan and cook the onion over a gentle heat until it is transparent but not browned. Add the kidneys and stir-fry over a medium heat for 3-4 minutes or until the blood has stopped running. Do not overcook the kidneys or they will become tough and rubbery.
4 Remove the kidneys from the pan with a slotted spoon and keep warm. Add the stock and port to the pan and allow to bubble over a high heat until the liquid is reduced by half. Stir occasionally to mix in the sediment from the bottom of the pan. Turn down heat to medium and add the mustard and jelly. Season to taste with salt and pepper. Cook for 2 minutes, stirring, until the jelly has melted and blended in. Add the cream and cook for 2-3 minutes more.
5 To serve, place a hot pastry basket in the centre of each of 6 heated plates. Pile in the kidneys and pour over the sauce. Arrange the vegetables around the plate and serve immediately.

Watercress, orange and fennel salad

6 small oranges, peeled and thinly
sliced
2 small or 1 large head of fennel,
outer leaves removed, thinly
sliced

1 bunch watercress, washed,
picked over and thoroughly
drained
juice of 1 orange
hazelnut, walnut or olive oil
salt and pepper

1 Arrange a circle of orange slices on each of 6 plates. Arrange a portion of fennel and watercress on top of these.

2 Sprinkle with the orange juice. Drizzle over a little oil and season to taste with salt and pepper.

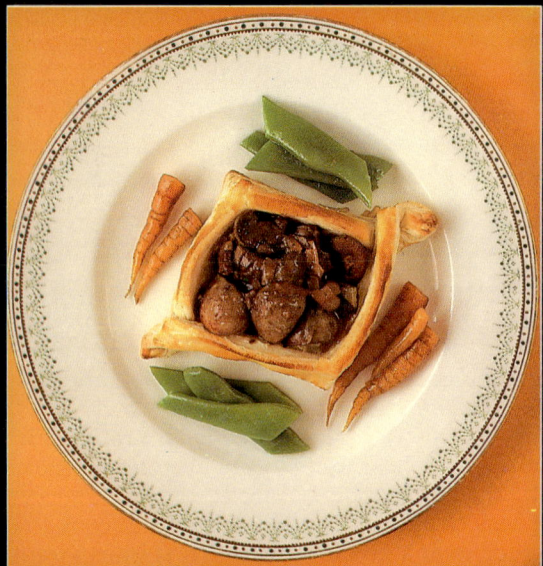

Above: Terrine of smoked fish with whisky prawn sauce
Right: Lambs' kidneys with port in puff pastry baskets
Below: Watercress, orange and fennel salad

Above: Spinach and smoked salmon roulade
Left: Yellow ragoût of seafood
Below: Spiced steamed puddings with ginger sauce

Spinach and smoked salmon roulade

•

Yellow ragoût of seafood

•

Spiced steamed puddings with ginger sauce

Spinach and smoked salmon roulade

575 g/1¼ lb frozen spinach
25 g/1 oz butter, melted
5 eggs, separated
grated rind of ½ small lemon
grated nutmeg

salt and pepper
30 ml/2 tbsp freshly grated
*   Parmesan cheese*
125 g/4 oz thinly sliced smoked
*   salmon*
thin, seeded tomato slices or
*   watercress sprigs*

1 Butter a Swiss roll tin and line with well-buttered greaseproof paper, snipping the corners to make it fit and allowing the paper to stand up a little above the rim of the tin.
2 Cook the spinach according to the instructions on the packet. Drain well and purée in a food processor or blender.
3 In a large bowl, mix the spinach purée with the melted butter, egg yolks, grated lemon rind, a little grated nutmeg, and salt and pepper to taste.
4 Beat the egg whites until stiff. Whisk a spoonful or two of the whites into the spinach mixture, then fold in the remainder. Gently spoon the mixture into the lined tin, smoothing it into the corners. Bake on the second shelf in a preheated 200°C/400°F/Gas 6 oven for 12-15 minutes or until the mixture is set.
5 Turn onto a teatowel, sprinkled with the Parmesan. Arrange the smoked salmon slices evenly over the surface. Sprinkle with a few twists of pepper and roll up with the help of the teatowel to make a Swiss roll shape. Allow to cool in the teatowel.
6 To serve, place a thick slice on each of 6 plates. Garnish with tomato slices or watercress.

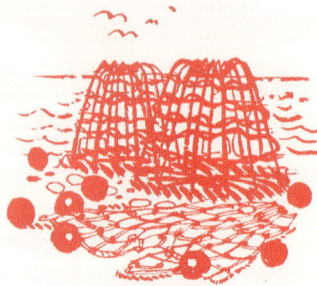

Yellow ragoût of seafood

225 g/8 oz shelled broad beans
  (fresh or frozen)
50 g/2 oz butter, melted
salt and pepper
15 ml/1 tbsp vegetable oil
15 ml/1 tbsp chopped onion
300 ml/½ pint single cream

15 ml/1 tbsp chopped fresh parsley
5 ml/1 tsp turmeric
700 g/1½ lb smoked cod or
  haddock fillets, skinned and cut
  into bite-size pieces
100 g/4 oz peeled cooked prawns,
  thawed if frozen
100 g/4 oz cockles, cooked and
  shelled (see page 30)

1 Cook the broad beans in boiling, salted water until just tender. When ready, drain, toss in the melted butter and sprinkle with black pepper to taste.
2 While the beans are cooking, heat the oil in a frying pan and cook the onion over a medium heat until transparent. Add the cream, parsley, turmeric and salt and pepper to taste. Bring to the simmer, stirring. Add the fish pieces and poach for 2 minutes, turn-ing once. Add the prawns and cockles and continue to cook, stirring very gently so as not to break up the fish, for a few seconds, just to coat the prawns and cockles with the sauce.
3 To serve, divide the fish and sauce between 6 hot plates and place a serving of broad beans next to this.
Note: Another vegetable can be substituted for the broad beans.

Spiced steamed puddings with ginger sauce

225 g/8 oz self-raising flour
25 ml/4 rounded tsp ground mixed
  spice
225 g/8 oz butter, softened
225 g/8 oz caster sugar
4 eggs

The sauce
30 ml/2 tbsp honey
250 ml/8 fl oz geen ginger wine
4 pieces stem ginger, chopped
30 ml/2 tbsp syrup from the jar of
  stem ginger
15 ml/1 tbsp lemon juice
10 ml/2 tsp arrowroot, dissolved in
  a little water

1 Mix the flour and ground spice. Cream the butter and sugar together until light and fluffy. Beat in the eggs one at a time, adding a heaped spoonful of the flour after each egg to prevent curdling. Mix in the remaining flour.
2 Butter 6 individual pudding moulds and spoon in the mixture so that the moulds are half filled. Cover the top of each mould tightly with a circle of foil. Steam over boiling water for 50 minutes.
3 Meanwhile place the honey, wine, ginger pieces, syrup and lemon juice in a small pan and bring to a gentle simmer. Thicken with the arrowroot, stirring well.
4 To serve, cut the tops level and turn out the puddings on to 6 heated plates and pour over the sauce.

A SPRING PALETTE

Suddenly, after the long dark months, mother nature begins to freshen up the countryside with her spring palette. Trees come to life as washes of brilliant green are laid one on top of the other. Primroses and violets follow the snowdrops. Buttercups and daisies add splashes of brightness to the hedgerows and meadows. Soon floods of colour fill the woods in drifts of sweet-scented bluebells.

The new warm-earth smells of spring coax us from our winter hibernation and out into the countryside. Our tastebuds yearn for the lightness and freshness of the first vegetables. Country walks provide young nettle tops for tasty soups and sauces. Baby dandelion leaves and wild sorrel add a sharp note to the taste of spring salads, and wild flowers add a little enchantment to the appearance of our food.

Primavera salad

●

Fresh pasta with three kinds of mushrooms

●

Cardamom-scented rhubarb fool

Primavera salad

2 bunches watercress, washed,
  picked over and thoroughly
  drained
30 ml/2 tbsp mayonnaise (see
  pages 20, 35)
30 ml/2 tbsp plain yogurt
225 g/8 oz mozzarella cheese, cut
  into julienne strips (see page 25)
24 fresh quails' eggs,
  hard-boiled, shelled and halved
approx. 30 primrose flowers and
  30 leaves

1 Make a nest-like circle around the edge of each plate with watercress.
2 Mix together the mayonnaise and yogurt and fold in the cheese. Place an equal amount of the cheese mixture in the centre of each plate.

3 Arrange 8 egg halves on each plate and scatter the flowers and leaves over.
4 Serve at room temperature but do not assemble too far in advance as the flowers and leaves may wilt.

Fresh pasta with three kinds of mushrooms

25 g/1 oz butter
1 medium onion, peeled and finely
chopped
75 g/3 oz dried mushrooms,
soaked, drained and chopped (see
page 32)
1 (425 g/15 oz) tin Chinese straw
mushrooms, drained (see page
34)

125 g/4 oz fresh button
mushrooms, finely sliced
1 clove garlic, peeled and crushed
300 ml/½ pint single cream
salt and pepper
about 600 g/1¼ lb fresh
tagliatelle (see pages 18, 32)
1 truffle, fresh or tinned, finely
chopped (optional)

1 Melt the butter in a saucepan and cook the onion until transparent. Add all the mushrooms and the garlic. Cover and cook gently for 5 minutes.
2 Add the cream and season with salt and pepper to taste. Simmer gently, covered, for 5 minutes.

3 Meanwhile, cook the pasta in a large pan of boiling water. Drain.
4 Divide the cooked pasta between 6 heated plates and spoon the sauce over. Garnish with chopped truffled if used.

Cardamom-scented rhubarb fool

450 g/1 lb rhubarb, roughly
chopped
175 g/6 oz sugar
grated rind and juice of 1 orange
10 cardamom pods, lightly
crushed
150 ml/¼ pint plain yogurt
300 ml/½ pint double cream,
whipped

1 Place the rhubarb, sugar, orange rind and juice and the cardamom pods in a heavy-bottomed saucepan. Cook, over a low heat, stirring occasionally, until the rhubarb has broken down to a mush. Remove and discard the cardamom pods.
2 You should have a reasonably thick purée.

If the fruit is still very runny, place a sieve over a bowl and allow some of the juice to drain away. Chill the fruit mixture.
3 Stir in the yogurt and fold in the whipped cream.
4 Pour into 6 individual serving glasses or bowls, or one large one. Serve chilled.

Below: Primavera salad

Left: Fresh pasta with three kinds of mushrooms

Right: Cardamom-scented rhubarb fool

Hot vegetable bundles with nettle sauce and garlic croûtons

●

Pan-fried marinated lamb with leek and lemon sauce and rice timbales

●

Gingered caramel creams

Hot vegetable bundles with nettle sauce and garlic croûtons

225 g/8 oz carrots, peeled
225 g/8 oz celery
225 g/8 oz parsnips (or swedes or
turnips), peeled

The sauce
50 g/2 oz butter
1 medium onion, peeled and
chopped
about 200 g/7 oz fresh stinging
nettle tops (see page 33)

2 cloves garlic, peeled and crushed
60 ml/4 tbsp pale stock (see page 19)
salt and pepper
60 ml/4 tbsp single cream

The croûtons
75 g/3 oz butter
3 slices white bread, crusts
removed, cut into small cubes
1 clove garlic, peeled and crushed

1 First make the sauce. Melt the butter in a saucepan and cook the onion over a low heat until it is transparent. Add the nettles, garlic and stock and season with salt and pepper to taste. Cover the pan and cook over low heat for 10-15 minutes or until the nettles are completely wilted.
2 Meanwhile, prepare the croûtons. Melt the butter in a frying pan, add the bread cubes and garlic and cook over a low heat, turning constantly, until the croûtons are crisp and golden. Drain on kitchen paper and set aside.
3 Place the sauce in a food processor or blender and add the cream. Blend until the sauce is smooth. Pour back into the saucepan and reheat gently.
4 Meanwhile cut the vegetables into even sticks, about 7.5 cm/3 inches long and 5 mm/¼ inch wide. Steam separately until just tender.
5 Arrange the bundles of vegetables on heated plates. Spoon over the sauce and sprinkle with the croûtons.
Note: Any seasonal vegetables may be used, eg beans, asparagus, mange touts, etc.

Pan-fried marinated lamb with leek and lemon sauce and rice timbales

45 ml/3 tbsp olive oil
30 ml/2 tbsp lemon juice
3 cloves garlic, peeled and crushed
10 ml/2 tsp chopped fresh
rosemary, or 5 ml/1 tsp dried
rosemary if fresh is not available
pepper
700 g/1½ lb lean, boneless lamb,
from the leg, cut into small cubes

425 g/15 oz long-grain rice, freshly
cooked (see page 34)
2 spring onions, finely chopped,
including green part
finely chopped fresh mint (do not
substitute dried, omit if
unavailable)
finely chopped fresh parsley

The sauce
25 g/1 oz butter
450 g/1 lb leeks, trimmed and
coarsely chopped
grated rind and juice of 1 lemon
90 ml/6 tbsp pale stock (see page 19)
salt and pepper

1 Mix together 30 ml/2 tbsp of the oil, the lemon juice, garlic, rosemary and a few twists of pepper in a mixing bowl. Add the lamb cubes and mix well to make sure all the pieces are coated with the marinade. Cover and leave to marinate overnight, or for 12 to 24 hours.

2 To make the sauce, melt the butter in a saucepan and cook the leeks over a gentle heat for 5 minutes. Add the lemon rind and juice and the stock and season to taste with salt and pepper. Cover the pan and cook for 10 minutes.

3 Meanwhile, drain the lamb cubes. Heat the remaining oil in a large frying pan and fry the lamb over a medium heat until just cooked, 5-10 minutes. Turn the lamb cubes frequently so that they brown evenly.

4 Tip the sauce into a blender or food processor and blend until completely smooth. If the sauce seems too thick, add a little water. Return to the saucepan and reheat.

5 To serve, press the cooked rice firmly into 6 well-buttered timbales or dariole moulds, and turn out onto hot plates. Place the meat next to the rice and spoon over the sauce. Sprinkle with the chopped onion and herbs. Hot pitta bread makes a good accompaniment to this dish.

Gingered caramel creams

4 whole eggs
2 egg yolks
50 g/2 oz granulated sugar
10 ml/2 tsp ground ginger
300 ml/½ pint milk
300 ml/½ pint single cream

6 pieces preserved stem ginger in
*   syrup cut in halves*

The caramel
125 g/4 oz granulated sugar
30 ml/2 tbsp water

1 Make the caramel by heating the sugar with the water in a small pan over a medium heat until dissolved. Do not stir, but continue to cook until the mixture is a deep golden brown. Remove from the heat immediately and pour into the bottom of 6 dampened ovenproof dishes. Working very quickly as the caramel soon hardens, tilt each dish to make sure the bottom is coated with caramel. Set aside.

2 Whisk the eggs and egg yolks with the sugar and ground ginger until white and smooth. Heat the milk and cream together in a saucepan until just below boiling and pour in a steady stream onto the egg mixture, whisking constantly. Strain through a sieve.

3 Pour into the dishes and cover each with foil. Cook in a bain-marie (see page 24) in a preheated 180°C/350°F/Gas 4 oven for 40 minutes. Allow to cool, then chill in the refrigerator.

4 To serve, run a knife around the edge of each cream to loosen it, then turn out onto cold plates. Garnish with the preserved ginger.

*Above: Hot vegetable bundles with
nettle sauce and garlic croûtons
Right: Pan-fried marinated lamb
with leek and lemon sauce and rice
timbales
Left: Gingered caramel creams*

Saucy little tarts

●

Smokey topaz chicken

●

Salad of bitter leaves

Saucy little tarts

*12 small square puff pastry baskets
    (see page 23)*
*100 g/4 oz carrots, peeled and cut
    into julienne strips (see page 25)*
50 g/2 oz butter
pinch of sugar
*small pinch of rosemary, fresh or
    dried*
salt and pepper
4 eggs
15 ml/1 tbsp single cream
15 ml/1 tbsp pale stock (see page 19)
5 ml/1 tsp lemon juice
1 egg yolk, beaten

The sauces
25 g/1 oz butter
*1 small onion, peeled and finely
    chopped*
1 clove garlic, peeled and crushed
*450 g/1 lb tomatoes, peeled, seeded
    and chopped*
pinch of dried oregano
pinch of sugar
15 ml/1 tbsp white wine
salt and pepper
*½ bunch watercress, washed, picked
    over and thoroughly dried*
150 ml/¼ pint double cream

1 To make the sauces: melt the butter in a saucepan and cook the onion and garlic over a medium heat until transparent. Add the tomatoes, oregano, sugar, wine and salt and pepper to taste and cook on a medium heat for 4 minutes. Purée the sauce in a blender or food processor, then return to the saucepan ready for reheating.

2 Purée the watercress with the cream in the blender or food processor and season with salt to taste. Put into a saucepan ready to heat.

3 Cook the carrots in boiling salted water for 3 minutes. Drain and return to the pan. Add half of the butter, sugar, rosemary and salt and pepper to taste and cook for 5 minutes.

4 Reheat the tomato sauce. Heat the watercress sauce gently to just below boiling point.

5 Mix the whole eggs lightly with the cream and season to taste with salt and pepper. Scramble very lightly in the remaining butter.

6 Mix together the stock, lemon juice and egg yolk. Pour the mixture onto the hot carrots, cover and shake the pan gently. This will coat the carrots with sauce, the heat from the carrots just cooking the egg.

7 To serve, fill half the puff pastry baskets with the carrot mixture and half with the scrambled egg. Divide the sauces between 6 hot plates, keeping them separate. Arrange one of each basket on each plate. Serve warm.

Smokey topaz chicken

6 small slices of smoked ham
6 chicken breast fillets, flattened
  (see page 27)
1 (375 g/13 oz) jar stem ginger in
  syrup
salt
large pot of strong Lapsang
  Souchong tea, strained
10 ml/2 tsp arrowroot, dissolved
  in a little water
freshly cooked seasonal
  vegetables

1 Place a slice of ham on each piece of chicken. Finely chop 2 pieces of the ginger and divide between the pieces of ham. Roll up each breast tightly and secure with wooden cocktail sticks (see page 27).
2 Place the rolls in a saucepan just large enough to fit them in one layer. Sprinkle with a little salt and pour over enough tea just to cover. Bring to the boil and simmer for just 5 minutes. Remove the chicken rolls with a slotted spoon. Remove all the cocktail sticks and keep the rolls warm.

3 Over a fierce heat, boil the liquid in the pan until reduced to 150 ml/¼ pint. Add the syrup from the ginger jar and thicken with the arrowroot. Keep warm.
4 Cut the chicken rolls crossways into 1-cm/½-inch slices and arrange on hot plates. Spoon over a little of the hot sauce and garnish with more ginger pieces. Add the vegetables to the plates and serve hot.

Salad of bitter leaves

2 bunches watercress, washed,
  picked over and thoroughly
  drained
handful of tiny dandelion leaves,
  washed and drained
3 oranges, peeled and cut into
  segments (see page 27)
salt and pepper
walnut, hazelnut or olive oil

1 Mix all the leaves together and place in an attractive serving bowl or divide between 6 plates or bowls.
2 Arrange the orange segments over the salad. Season with salt and pepper to taste and sprinkle very lightly with the oil of your choice.

Left: Saucy little tarts
Below: Smokey topaz chicken
Above: Salad of bitter leaves

Above: Avocado and grapefruit salad with smoked mussels
Right: Rabbit pies with olives and grapes
Below: Coffee custards with chocolate and whisky sauce

Avocado and grapefruit salad with smoked mussels

●

Rabbit pies with olives and grapes

●

Coffee custards with chocolate and whisky sauce

Avocado and grapefruit salad with smoked mussels

2 large or 3 small ripe avocado
pears
juice of 1 lemon
2 large grapefruits, peeled and cut
into thin slices
1 (105 g/4 oz) tin smoked mussels
in vegetable oil, drained

1 Peel the avocados, cut in half and carefully removed the stones. Cut the flesh into thin slices lengthways, and put in a bowl with the lemon juice. Toss gently to make sure that each slice is well coated. This will stop the avocado discolouring.

2 Arrange some of the grapefruit slices on each plate, and then add a fan of avocado slices. Garnish with the smoked mussels.
Note: Salt and pepper are not necessary, but may be added if liked.

Rabbit pies with olives and grapes

60 ml/4 tbsp olive oil
1.5 kg/3 lb rabbit joints
1 clove garlic, peeled and crushed
1 stick celery, finely sliced
300 ml/½ pint white grape juice
(bottled or from a carton)
100 g/4 oz small black olives,
stoned
salt and pepper
30 ml/2 tbsp concentrated tomato
purée

150 ml/½ pint pale stock (see
page 19)
100 g/4 oz small seedless green
grapes
basic shortcrust pastry no.2, made
with 100 g/4 oz flour (see page 20)
beaten egg yolk to glaze
freshly cooked seasonal
vegetables

1 In a saucepan large enough to take the rabbit joints in one layer (a lidded sauté pan is ideal), heat the oil. Add the rabbit, the garlic and celery. Cover the pan tightly and cook over a low heat, turning occasionally, for 1½ hours.

2 Uncover the pan. You will find that the meat will have given off a lot of juice. Turn up the heat and continue to cook uncovered until all the liquid has evaporated.

3 Add the grape juice and olives and season to taste with salt and pepper. Cook over a high heat until all the grape juice has evaporated.

4 Mix the tomato purée with the stock and add to the pan with the grapes. Cook for 5 minutes.

5 Meanwhile, roll out the pastry thinly, and cut out 6 7.5-cm/3-3½-inch discs using a pastry cutter. Place on a greased and floured baking sheet. Brush the pastry discs with beaten egg yolk. Bake in a preheated 220°C/425°F/Gas 7 oven for 10-15 minutes or until crisp and golden. Keep warm.

6 To serve, divide the rabbit between 6 hot plates and spoon over the sauce, with the olives and grapes. Place a pastry disc over each serving and add the vegetables. Serve very hot.

Coffee custards with chocolate and whisky sauce

3 eggs
3 egg yolks
45 ml/3 tbsp caster sugar
30 ml/2 tbsp instant coffee
powder dissolved in 150 ml/
¼ pint water
150 ml/¼ pint single cream

The sauce
150 g/5 oz granulated sugar
175 ml/6 fl oz water
100 g/3½ oz good plain chocolate
15 ml/1 tbsp whisky (or more if
liked)

1 Whisk the eggs, egg yolks and sugar together until creamy. Heat the coffee with the cream to just below boiling point and pour in a steady stream onto the egg mixture, stirring all the time. Strain and pour into 6 dampened individual moulds.

2 Bake in a bain-marie (see page 24) in a preheated 180°C/350°F/Gas 4 oven for about 30 minutes, or until the point of a knife inserted into the custard comes out clean. Cool, then chill for at least 4 hours or overnight.

3 To make the sauce, dissolve the sugar in the water, then boil for 5 minutes over a medium heat to make a syrup. Add the chocolate, broken into small pieces, and stir until melted. Allow to cool, then add the whisky.

4 To serve, turn out the chilled custards onto 6 small plates and pour over the sauce.

Note: Cream for serving is not necessary but makes this dish even more deliciously rich.

Left: Spring vegetables in jellied Muscadet with herbed goat's cheese sauce
Above: Chillied chicken livers with pepper rice
Below: Polkadot puddings

Spring vegetables in jellied Muscadet with herbed goat's cheese sauce

●

Chillied chicken livers with pepper rice

●

Polkadot puddings

Spring vegetables in jellied Muscadet with herbed goat's cheese sauce

*600 ml/1 pint Muscadet, or other
  light dry white wine
20 ml/4 tsp powdered gelatine
5 ml/1 tsp salt
6 thin mushroom slices or 6
  asparagus tips, cooked
2 spring onions, thinly sliced
15 ml/1 tbsp small peas, cooked
15 ml/1 tbsp diced red pepper*

*1 small carrot, peeled and cut into
  very thin rings*

The sauce
*1 egg
2.5 ml/½ tsp dry mustard
salt and pepper
150 ml/¼ pint vegetable oil*

*5 ml/1 tsp lemon juice
15 ml/1 tbsp boiling water
100 g/4 oz goat's cheese (soft if
  possible)
20 ml/1 heaped tbsp chopped parsley
20 ml/1 heaped tbsp finely chopped
  green spring onion top*

1 Heat half the wine in a saucepan and sprinkle over the gelatine. Stir over a gentle heat until completely dissolved. Add to the rest of the wine in a large jug with the salt and stir well.

2 Pour a little wine jelly into the bottom of 6 dampened individual moulds and chill in the refrigerator until set.

3 Place a slice of mushroom or an asparagus tip on the set jelly in each mould and pour over some of the liquid jelly. Return to the refrigerator and chill until set. Continue in this way, arranging the different vegetables in layers of jelly, until the moulds are full. If the jelly in the jug begins to set before you are ready to use it, stand the jug in a bowl or pan of hot water.

4 Leave the jellies in the refrigerator for at least 6 hours or until firmly set.

5 To make the sauce, place the egg, mustard and a little salt and pepper in the container of a blender or food processor. With the motor running, pour on the oil in a very slow steady stream. This will form a thick mayonnaise. With the motor still running, add the lemon juice and boiling water, then the cheese, parsley and spring onion tops and process until smooth and well mixed. Do not over process as it is nice to see little green bits in the sauce.

6 To serve, dip each mould momentarily into boiling water and immediately invert onto a plate. A firm shake should release the jelly with a plop. If nothing happens the first time, dip the mould, again momentarily, into the boiling water and repeat the process.

7 Place a little of the cheese sauce on each plate and serve immediately.

Chillied chicken livers with pepper rice

15 ml/1 tbsp vegetable oil
25 g/1 oz butter
1 medium onion, peeled and
chopped
1 clove garlic, peeled and crushed
2.5-5 ml/½-1 tsp chilli powder
(or to taste)
salt and pepper
700 g/1½ lb chicken livers
15 ml/1 tbsp cornflour mixed with
300ml/½ pint water

green beans or other green vegetable
chopped parsley to garnish

The rice
30 ml/2 tbsp vegetable oil
generous 15 ml/1 tbsp chopped red
pepper
generous 15 ml/1 tbsp chopped
green pepper

5 ml/1 tsp green peppercorns
(see page 30), optional
1 clove garlic, peeled and crushed
500 g/18 oz basmati rice
(see page 34), washed
1.2 litres/2 pints water
salt

1 First prepare the rice. Heat the oil in a medium saucepan and cook the red and green peppers with the green peppercorns and garlic over a low heat for 5 minutes. Add the rice and cook for 5 more minutes, stirring constantly so that the rice is completely coated with the oil and until it has a slightly transparent look. Add the water, and season with salt to taste. Give the contents of the pan a good stir. Bring to the boil, then turn down the heat to a slow simmer and tightly cover the pan. Cook for 15 minutes or until the water is completely absorbed by the rice, and the rice is cooked.
2 Meanwhile, cook the livers. Heat the oil with the butter in a large frying pan and cook the onion over a medium heat until transparent. Add the garlic and season with the chilli powder and salt and pepper to taste. Cook for 2 minutes more, then add the chicken livers. Cook, stirring constantly, until the chicken livers are almost cooked. Add the cornflour and water and cook for 1-2 minutes more or until the gravy has thickened and the livers are cooked. Do not overcook as the livers will toughen.
3 At the same time, cook the green beans.
4 Press the rice into 6 buttered moulds.
5 To serve, unmould the rice or simply spoon onto the heated plates. Add the livers, sauce and beans. Sprinkle with parsley.

Polkadot puddings

100 g/4 oz butter, at room
temperature
100 g/4 oz caster sugar
2 eggs
75 g/3 oz self-raising flour

50 g/2 oz ground almonds
1 (425 g/15 oz) tin red cherries,
stoned, drained and juice reserved

The sauce
2 egg yolks
25 g/1 oz caster sugar
a little Maraschino or cherry
brandy

1 Cream the butter with the sugar until light and fluffy. Beat in the eggs one at a time, adding 15 ml/1 tbsp of flour with each egg to prevent curdling. Mix the remaining flour with the ground almonds and fold into the mixture.
2 Butter 12 small or 6 medium metal moulds and arrange some of the cherries in the bottom of each mould. Spoon in the batter so that the moulds are only just over half full.
3 Bake in a preheated 190°C/375°F/Gas 5 oven for 20 minutes or until the puddings are golden and light.
4 Meanwhile, make the sauce. Put the egg yolks and sugar in a basin over boiling water and whisk over a gentle heat until the mixture starts to foam. Add 150 ml/¼ pint of the reserved cherry juice a little at a time, whisking continuously. Keep the sauce warm over hot water; do not allow it to get any hotter. Just before serving, whisk in the liqueur.
5 The puddings should have risen just above the top of the moulds, so slice off the sponges level with the mould top to make flat bases for the puddings when turned out.
6 Place one or two puddings on each plate and pour on the sauce.

SUMMER RICHNESS

Tea on the lawn, the noise of bat on ball, the smell of new mown grass are all signs of summer.
The land is now at its most bountiful and provides all the food we need for summer eating. We need no longer rely on imported produce which was so welcome in the colder months. Delicious meals are quickly and effortlessly prepared. Uncomplicated dishes allow the simple natural flavours of fresh, home-grown ingredients to speak for themselves.

English vegetables are available in abundance. The sharp taste of rhubarb and gooseberries is quickly followed by the lush juicy sweetness of soft summer fruits such as strawberries, raspberries and currants. Salmon and trout are now at their best and cheapest.

These superb ingredients need but the simplest cooking. The addition of some fresh homegrown herbs provides all we need for memorable summer dinner parties. Time saved in the kitchen can be spent out of doors – perhaps with a pre-dinner drink enjoying the company of friends and the summer sunshine.

Hot ham mousse with tomato sauce

●

Risotto of red summer vegetables

●

Redcurrant summer pudding

Hot ham mousse with tomato sauce

225 g/8 oz cooked ham
2 eggs
2 egg yolks
350 ml/12 fl oz double cream
5 ml/1 tsp dry English mustard
salt and pepper
6 small shapes cut from a thin
   slice of cooked ham

The sauce
15 ml/1 tbsp olive oil
1 small onion, peeled and chopped
450 g/1 lb tomatoes, roughly
   chopped
pinch of dried thyme
1.25 ml/¼ tsp fennel seed
salt and pepper

1 Place the ham in the container of a blender or food processor and process until very finely minced. Add the eggs, egg yolks, cream, mustard, and salt and pepper to taste and process until just amalgamated. If the mixture becomes foamy, leave in the refrigerator until the foam disappears.
2 Generously butter 6 ramekin dishes or other individual moulds. Fill the moulds not quite to the top with the ham mixture and cover each with a small circle of greased foil. Place in a bain-marie (see page 24) and bake in a preheated 190°C/375°F/Gas 5 oven for 35 minutes or until a knife point inserted in the middle of a mousse comes out clean.
3 Meanwhile, make the sauce. Heat the oil in

a small pan and cook the onion until transparent. Add the tomatoes with the thyme, fennel and a little salt and pepper. Be careful with the salt as the ham might already contain enough salt. Cover and cook over a gentle heat for 5-10 minutes or until the tomatoes have turned into a mush.
4 Press the sauce through a wire sieve with the back of a wooden spoon and discard any solids left in the sieve. Reheat the sauce.
5 To serve, run a small knife around the edge of each mousse and carefully turn out onto 6 hot plates. Surround with the sauce and decorate with the ham shapes. Hand round thin slices of brown bread and butter.

Risotto of red, summer vegetables

50 g/2 oz butter
15 ml/1 tbsp vegetable oil
1 large onion, peeled and chopped
2 cloves garlic, peeled and
   crushed
425 g/15 oz arborio rice
   (see page 34)
1.8 litres/3 pints chicken or
   vegetable stock (see page 19)

1 red pepper, cored, seeded and
   finely chopped
225 g/8 oz cooked beetroot, peeled
   and diced
225 g/8 oz tomatoes, skinned,
   seeded and diced (see page 25)
salt and pepper
175 g/6 oz shelled broad beans
   (frozen if fresh are not available)

1 Melt the butter in a large saucepan and add the oil. Cook the onion until transparent. Add the garlic and rice, and continue to cook, stirring constantly, for 5 minutes until the rice is well coated with fat and is shiny.

2 Meanwhile, in another saucepan, bring the stock to the boil. Ladle enough of the simmering stock onto the rice just to cover. Keep cooking the rice over a moderate heat, stirring continuously, until all the liquid has been absorbed. Ladle on more stock and continue cooking until the rice is tender, 20-25 minutes. Add more stock as each batch is absorbed. The finished risotto should be quite wet and creamy, but with a little bite left in the middle of each grain of rice. This process might not use all the stock, or it may all be used up before the rice is fully cooked, in which case add some boiling water.

3 About 2-3 minutes before the rice is cooked, stir in the red pepper, beetroot and tomatoes. By the time the rice is fully cooked, the vegetables will be hot, but the pepper will still be very crunchy. Season to taste with salt and pepper.

4 At the last minute, steam the broad beans until just tender.

5 To serve, spoon the risotto onto hot plates or into soup bowls and garnish with the broad beans.

Note: Do not add Parmesan cheese as this would overpower the delicate flavour of this dish.

Redcurrant summer pudding

100 g/4 oz sugar
900 g/2 lbs redcurrants, removed
from stems, washed and drained
30-45 ml/2-3 tbsp Cointreau or
other fruit liqueur
½-¾ sliced white loaf, crusts
removed, each slice halved

1 Sprinkle the sugar over the fruit and add the liqueur. Mix gently and leave to macerate at room temperature for 1 hour for the juices to flow.

2 Carefully line a large pudding bowl with slices of bread, overlapping the slices only enough to cover the inside of the bowl. Add enough fruit to come halfway up the bowl. Cover with a layer of bread, then fill almost to the top with the rest of the fruit. (If there is any fruit left over it may be served with the pudding, separately.) Cover the bowl with more bread. Place a small plate, just big enough to fit inside the rim of the bowl, on top of the top layer of bread and place a weight on top of this (a jar of jam is ideal). Leave in the refrigerator for several hours, or overnight.

3 To serve, turn out onto your prettiest plate. Slice in wedges and serve with lightly whipped cream.

Above: Hot ham mousse with tomato sauce
Right: Risotto of red summer vegetables
Left: Redcurrant summer pudding

Asparagus custards
●
Grilled trout with new potatoes in orange butter
●
Strawberries in raspberry sauce

Asparagus custards

450 g/1 lb asparagus, trimmed
3 eggs, lightly beaten
120 ml/4 fl oz double cream
salt and pepper
100 g/4 oz clarified butter
  (see page 25)
1 clove garlic, peeled and finely
  sliced

1 Remove the tips from the asparagus stalks and set aside. Cook the stems in boiled salted water until tender, about 10 minutes. At the same time, steam the tips in a steamer arranged over the saucepan. Drain, keeping stems and tips separate.
2 Place the cooked stems in the container of a blender or food processor with the eggs, cream and salt and pepper to taste and process until smooth. Do not over process or the mixture will become frothy.
3 Pour the asparagus custard into 6 well-buttered ramekin dishes and float some of the asparagus tips on the top of each. Cover each dish with a small round of buttered foil. Bake in a bain-marie (see page 24) in a preheated 190°C/375°F/Gas 5 oven for 35 minutes.
4 Meanwhile, heat the butter in a small saucepan. Add the garlic and cook over a low heat for a few minutes, being careful that the garlic does not burn. When the butter is well-flavoured remove the garlic with a slotted spoon.
5 To serve, place the hot custards in their dishes on 6 individual serving plates. Pour some of the hot, garlic-flavoured butter over each custard and serve immediately.

Grilled trout with new potatoes in orange butter

6 medium trout, cleaned but with
heads and tails left on
100 g/4 oz butter, melted
salt and pepper
18 small, thin orange slices
0.9-1.35 kg/2-3 lb new potatoes,
scrubbed (Jerseys if available)
100 g/4 oz clarified butter (see page
25)
grated rind of 1 large orange
freshly cooked seasonal vegetables

1 Brush the fish inside and out with melted butter and season with salt and pepper. Place 3 slices of orange inside each fish. Cook under a preheated grill for 5-7 minutes each side.
2 Meanwhile, boil or steam the potatoes until cooked. Drain.

3 Heat the clarified butter with the orange rind and toss the potatoes in this until well coated. Season with salt and pepper.
4 To serve, place a trout on each plate and accompany with the vegetables, pouring over any remaining orange butter.

Strawberries in raspberry sauce

225 g/8 oz raspberries
25 g/1 oz caster sugar
30 ml/2 tbsp fresh orange juice
900 g/2 lb strawberries, hulled,
washed and well drained
150 ml/¼ pint double cream,
lightly whipped

1 Place the raspberries in the container of a blender or food processor with the sugar and orange juice and blend until smooth. Strain through a fine sieve to remove seeds, and chill.
2 To serve, pile the strawberries in 6 pretty

dishes and pour over the chilled raspberry sauce. Top with the whipped cream.
Note: This tastes best if the strawberries are at room temperature, with the cream and sauce served chilled.

Above: Asparagus custards
Right: Strawberries in raspberry
sauce

Watercress and orange soup

●

Chicken with almond sauce and sesame beans

●

Summer fruit symphony

Watercress and orange soup

*1.8 litres/3 pints chicken stock
  (see page 19)
juice of 2 large oranges
1 bunch watercress, washed,
  picked over and thoroughly
  drained
salt and pepper
6 orange slices*

1 Heat the stock with the orange juice and, when simmering, add the watercress. Continue to simmer for 1-2 minutes or just until the stems of the watercress are softened.
2 Check for seasoning. Do not overseason this delicately flavoured soup.

3 To serve, pour into heated soup bowls or plates and float an orange slice on each serving.

Chicken with almond sauce and sesame beans

1 boiled chicken (see page 31)
300 ml/½ pint milk
1 small onion, peeled and
   quartered
salt and pepper
75 g/3 oz fresh white
   breadcrumbs
100 g/4 oz ground almonds
300 ml/½ pint or more chicken
   stock (see page 19)
1 clove garlic, peeled and crushed
75 g/3 oz butter
450 g/1 lb or more green beans
15 ml/1 tbsp sesame seeds
50 g/2 oz blanched almond halves,
   toasted (see page 25)

1 If the chicken has been cooked previously, reheat it in a steamer over a pan of boiling water.
2 To make the sauce, place the milk and onion in a saucepan and season with salt and pepper. Bring to the boil and simmer over a very low heat for 15 minutes. Remove from the heat. Add the breadcrumbs and almonds, stir well and leave to soak for 30 minutes.
3 Meanwhile, cut the chicken meat from the carcass, discard the skin, and cut the meat into small slices. Keep warm in a dish in the oven, covered with foil.
4 Place the contents of the saucepan in the container of a blender or food processor and add the stock and garlic. Blend until smooth. Reheat in a saucepan with 25 g/1 oz of the butter. If the sauce seems too thick, add a little more stock. Keep hot.
5 Steam the beans until just cooked. Meanwhile, heat the remaining butter in a saucepan and cook the sesame seeds over a low heat for a few minutes until they turn golden. Drain the beans and toss in the sesame seed butter.
6 To serve, divide the chicken between 6 hot plates and spoon over some of the almond sauce. Sprinkle with the toasted almonds. Divide out the beans and serve immediately.

Summer fruit symphony

18 medium strawberries, washed
   and dried
100-175 g/4-6 oz raspberries
100-175 g/4-6 oz redcurrants,
   removed from stalks, washed and
   dried
24 ripe cherries, washed and dried
1 large or 2 small peaches, stoned
   and cut into segments
6 puff pastry butterflies (see page
   23)

1 Make an attractive arrangement of the fruit on 6 pretty plates and garnish with the pastry shapes.
Note: It is nice to leave stalks on fruit wherever possible so that they can be eaten by hand. This recipe allows for quantities and types of fruit to be varied according to taste and season.

Left: Watercress and orange soup
Below: Chicken with almond sauce
and sesame beans
Right: Summer fruit symphony

Green bean and walnut salad

●

Salmon steaks poached in cream with cucumber

●

Gooseberry tart with almond pastry

Green bean and walnut salad

700 g/1½ lb green beans, steamed
until just tender, drained and
chilled
100 g/4 oz shelled walnut halves
walnut oil (or other nut or olive oil)
lemon juice
salt and pepper

1 Divide the chilled beans between 6 chilled plates. Arrange the walnut halves on top.
2 Drizzle with oil and lemon juice and sprinkle over a little salt and pepper to taste.

Note: This salad is even nicer if the beans are made up of several varieties, eg runners, bobby and Kenya.

Salmon steaks poached in cream with cucumber

450 ml/¾ pint single cream
7.5-cm/3-inch piece cucumber, cut
in julienne strips (see page 25)
salt and pepper
6 salmon steaks

1 Place the cream and cucumber in a wide, shallow pan just large enough to fit the salmon steaks in one layer. Heat to simmering point and season with salt and pepper to taste.
2 Add the fish and cook over a gentle heat, turning just once, for about 5-10 minutes, depending on the thickness of the steaks.
3 To serve, place a steak on each heated plate and spoon over the cucumber cream sauce. Accompany with buttered, steamed new potatoes.

Gooseberry tart with almond pastry

700 g/1½ lb gooseberries, topped
and tailed
100 g/4 oz sugar
almond pastry, made with 100 g/4
oz flour (see page 21)
300 ml/½ pint double cream,
whipped until stiff

1 Place the gooseberries and sugar in a heavy-bottomed saucepan. Cover the pan and cook over a low heat only until the skins change colour and before any of the fruit burst. Shake the pan frequently during cooking. Remove from the heat and allow to cool.
2 Roll out the pastry thinly and use to line a large loose-bottomed 25-cm/10-inch flan tin. Bake blind in a preheated 220°C/425°F/Gas 7 oven for 20-25 minutes until crisp and golden (see page 25). Cool.
3 To assemble, fill the pastry case with the whipped cream and smooth the top with a knife. Arrange the gooseberries neatly in concentric circles over the cream. Serve as soon as possible after assembling.

Above: Green bean and walnut salad
Left: Salmon steaks poached in
cream with cucumber
Below: Gooseberry tart with almond
pastry

Above: Steamed buns with a chicken and cream cheese filling
Right: Cheese terrine with a salad of hot and cold vegetables
Below: Spiced rice pudding in biscuit baskets

Steamed buns with a chicken and cream cheese filling

•

Cheese terrine with a salad of hot and cold vegetables

•

Spiced rice pudding in biscuit baskets

Steamed buns with a chicken and cream cheese filling

*225 g/8 oz cooked chicken meat,
  finely chopped
30 ml/2 tbsp finely chopped
  spring onion, including green
  part
2 small gherkins, finely chopped
100 g/4 oz softened cream cheese
30 ml/2 tbsp single cream
salt and pepper
225 g/8 oz plain flour*

*3.75 ml/¾ tsp 'fast action' dried
  yeast (see page 34)
175 ml/6 fl oz milk, heated to
  blood temperature
6 spring onions, trimmed
6 small gherkins, fanned
  (see page 24)
a few long chives (if available)*

1 Mix together the chicken, chopped onion and gherkin, the cream cheese and cream, season well with salt and pepper, and set aside.
2 Mix the flour with 5 ml/½ tsp salt and the yeast. Mix in the milk. Turn onto a floured work surface and knead for 10 minutes. Form into a roll and cut into 6 equal portions. Roll out each portion to form a circle approximately 15 cm/6 inches in diameter.
3 Divide the chicken mixture between the dough circles, placing it in the centre. Dampen the edges of the circles, then bring up the edges, pleating them together to make

6 little 'sacks'. A final firm quarter twist will seal the tops.
4 Cut out a small circle of greaseproof paper to fit the bottom of each bun and grease with a little oil. Place the buns on the papers and arrange in a steamer, allowing at least 2.5 cm/1 inch of space between each bun. Set aside in a warm place to rise until doubled in size.
5 Place the steamer over boiling water and steam for 15 minutes.
6 Serve immediately, accompanied by whole spring onions, gherkin fans and chives (if used).

Cheese terrine with a salad of hot and cold vegetables

*225 g/8 oz Red Leicester cheese,
  coarsely chopped
300 ml/½ pint chicken or
  vegetable stock (see page 19)
generous 25 ml/5 tsp powdered
  gelatine
150 ml/¼ pint double cream,
  lightly whipped
1 egg white, whisked until stiff
  but not dry
½ pint/300 ml clear apple juice
2 spring onions, finely chopped,*

*including green part
1 large carrot, peeled and cut into
  julienne strips (see page 25)
1 small leek, trimmed and cut into
  julienne strips (see page 25)
1 medium courgette, cut into
  julienne strips (see page 25)
melted butter
pepper
¾ cucumber, cut into wafer-thin
  slices
½ box mustard and cress*

1 Place the cheese in the container of a blender or food processor with half the stock and process until smooth.

2 Heat the rest of the stock in a small saucepan and sprinkle over a generous 15 ml/3 tsp of the gelatine. Stir over a low heat until dissolved, then add to the cheese mixture. Blend again briefly.

3 Pour the mixture into a large bowl. Fold in first the cream and then the egg whites. Set aside.

4 Heat half the apple juice in a small saucepan and sprinkle on the remaining gelatine. Stir over a low heat until dissolved. Add to the rest of the apple juice and stir in the chopped spring onions.

5 Pour half the apple juice mixture into a dampened 900-ml/1½-pint loaf tin and chill in the refrigerator until completely set. Pour half the cheese mixture onto this layer. Return to the refrigerator and chill until set. Repeat, adding one more layer of each mixture. If either mixture should begin to set before needed, warm it over a bowl of hot water. Chill the terrine until completely set.

6 Just before serving, steam the julienne vegetables and toss in melted butter and pepper to taste.

7 Run a knife round the outside of the terrine. Dip the tin into boiling water for 1 second only, then invert onto a serving plate. The terrine should slip out evenly. If not, dip into boiling water for a further second, and repeat.

8 To serve, arrange the cucumber slices around the edge of each plate. Place a thick slice of terrine in the middle of each plate and surround with the warm julienne vegetables and the cress. Serve immediately.

Spiced rice pudding in biscuit baskets

75 g/3 oz pudding rice
900 ml/1½ pints creamy milk
75 g/3 oz sugar
25 g/1 oz dried mixed fruit
4 whole cloves
4 cardamom pods, lightly crushed
25 g/1 oz butter, cut into small
   pieces
julienne strips of orange rind (see
   page 25), blanched in boiling
   water for 5 minutes and well
   drained

The biscuits
100 g/4 oz butter
100 g/4 oz caster sugar
75 g/3 oz plain flour
2 egg whites
pinch of salt
2.5 ml/½ tsp vanilla essence

1 Butter a shallow ovenproof dish and place in it the rice, milk, sugar, dried fruit, cloves and cardamom pods. Dot the surface with small pieces of butter. Bake in a preheated 150°C/300°F/Gas 2 oven for 2½ hours or until all the liquid is absorbed and the rice is tender. Remove the whole spices, and chill the pudding.

2 Meanwhile, make the biscuit baskets. Cream together the butter and sugar until light and fluffy. Mix in the flour, egg whites, salt and vanilla essence. Allow the mixture to rest at room temperature for 30 minutes.

3 Butter 6 20-cm/8-inch rounds of greaseproof paper, and place two at a time on a baking sheet. Drop 15 ml/1 tbsp of the biscuit mixture into the centre of each of the two papers. Spread it out with the back of a spoon to make a smooth round, leaving a 2.5-cm/1-inch border of paper uncovered. Bake the biscuits two at a time on the top shelf of a preheated 180°C/350°F/Gas 4 oven for 10 minutes or until pale golden with a slightly browner edge.

4 Working quickly and very carefully, remove the biscuits from the oven and place each, top side down, over an upturned tumbler. Peel away the paper and press the biscuit down lightly around the glass on all sides to make a frilly cup shape. Remove from the tumbler when cool and firm. The biscuit baskets can be kept for several hours in an airtight container, but should be eaten as soon as possible after cooking to ensure crispness.

5 To serve, spoon the chilled rice pudding into the baskets and decorate with orange julienne.

A TASTE OF THE TROPICS

The holiday season is in full swing. Exotic dishes and outdoor meals prolong the holiday feeling, and bring home a taste of foreign lands. Even for those who have never left these shores, a taste of the tropics and a flavour of the mysterious east can be created at home, bringing a touch of glamour and excitement to late summer dinner parties.

These dishes borrow their flavours from many exotic lands – China and Japan, Malaysia and Indonesia. Everyday ingredients are combined with some less familiar ones in light, exciting and spicy combinations.

Original presentation will add to the exotic atmosphere of these tropically inspired menus so that, even when eaten in a garden, they suggest a flavour of the Far East. One might even imagine oneself, for a while perhaps, on an island in the South China Seas.

Curried pumpkin in coconut milk with noodles

●

Baked fish wrapped in leaves

●

Spiced banana salad

Curried pumpkin in coconut milk with noodles

15 ml/1 tbsp vegetable oil
*1 medium onion, peeled and finely
  chopped*
1 clove garlic, peeled and crushed
grated rind of ½ lemon
*5-cm/2-inch piece root ginger,
  peeled and finely chopped*
15 ml/1 tbsp good curry powder
5 ml/1 tbsp turmeric
*600 ml/1 pint coconut milk (see
  page 20)*

*700-900 g/1½-2 lb pumpkin,
  peeled and cut into 2.5-cm/1-inch
  cubes*
5 ml/1 tsp salt
*1 (225-g/8-oz) packet Chinese egg
  noodles*
150 ml/¼ pint plain yogurt
*15 ml/1 tbsp finely chopped
  coriander or parsley*

1 Heat the oil in a heavy-bottomed saucepan and cook the onion until transparent. Add the garlic, lemon rind, ginger and spices and stir-fry for 3 minutes. Stir in the coconut milk and continue to cook for 15 minutes over a gentle heat, stirring occasionally.
2 Meanwhile, sprinkle the pumpkin with the salt and steam until tender, about 15 minutes.

3 At the same time, cook the noodles according to the instructions on the packet.
4 Stir the yogurt into the sauce. Heat but do not allow to boil.
5 To serve, place a portion of noodles on each of 6 heated plates, add the steamed pumpkin and spoon over the sauce. Sprinkle with the chopped herb.

Baked fish wrapped in leaves

6 large cabbage leaves
vegetable oil
6 small red mullet or trout,
*   cleaned but head and tail left on*
salt and pepper
6 pinches of Chinese five-spice
*   powder*

12 small slivers root ginger
12 small slivers peeled garlic
18 thin peeled lemon slices
6 spring onions, halved
*   lengthways*

1 Drop the cabbage leaves, two at a time, into a large pan of rapidly boiling water and blanch until just wilted, 2-3 minutes. Drain, refresh in cold water and pat dry on kitchen paper towels. Brush the leaves with oil on both sides.
2 Season the fish inside and out with salt and pepper to taste and a pinch of five-spice powder. Place 2 slices each of garlic and ginger in the cavities.
3 Place 3 slices of lemon in a row on the centre of each cabbage leaf. Lay the fish on the lemon slices and place 2 long halves of onion along the top of each fish. Wrap the cabbage leaves around the fish to make neat parcels and secure with wooden cocktail sticks.
4 Place on a greased baking sheet and bake in a preheated 190°C/375°F/Gas 5 oven for about 20 minutes or until just cooked – the flesh of the fish will no longer look transparent.
5 To serve, place each fish on a hot plate and allow each guest to open his own parcel.

Spiced banana salad

40 g/1½ oz clarified butter (see
*   page 25)*
5 ml/1 tsp black cumin seed
1.25 ml/¼ tsp chilli powder
3 firm bananas, peeled and cut
*   into 1-cm/½-inch slices*
3 small heads chicory, washed and
*   separated into leaves*

1 medium, mild onion, peeled and
*   cut into very thin rings*
5 ml/1 tsp salt
150 ml/¼ pint plain yogurt
cayenne pepper

1 Heat the butter in a frying pan and fry the cumin and chilli powder over a medium heat for 2 minutes. Add the banana slices and fry for 2-3 minutes, turning once. The banana should be soft and hot but still hold its shape.
2 To serve, arrange the chicory leaves on 6 small plates or shallow bowls, radiating out from the centre. Add the onion rings and the warm banana and sprinkle with the salt. Top with the yogurt and sprinkle with the cayenne. Serve immediately.

Above: Curried pumpkin in coconut milk with noodles

Above: Baked fish wrapped in leaves
Right: Spiced banana salad

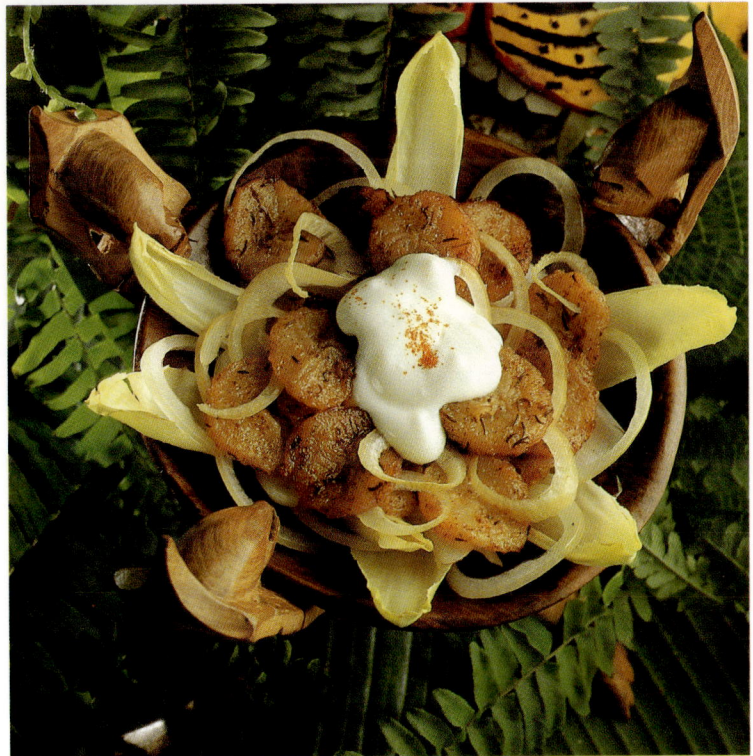

Oriental hors d'oeuvre

•

Chicken porcupine balls and sesame beef balls with okra

•

Oranges in green ginger wine

Oriental hors d'oeuvre

100 g/4 oz tiny mushrooms
15 ml/1 tbsp vegetable oil plus oil
  for cooking omelettes
15 ml/1 tbsp soy sauce
15-cm/6-inch piece cucumber, cut
  into 6 equal portions
50 g/2 oz white crabmeat (fresh or
  tinned)
50 g/2 oz cooked chopped
  spinach, cooled
salt and pepper

squeeze of lemon juice
2 eggs, beaten and seasoned with a
  dash of soy sauce
2 large or 4 small lettuce leaves,
  blanched and dried (see page 25)
6 big prawns, or several smaller
  ones, in their shells
6 (6 cm/2½ inch) squares of crisp
  lettuce, cut with scissors

1 Place the mushrooms, oil and soy sauce in a small saucepan with just enough water to cover. Bring to the boil and simmer for 10 minutes. Allow to cool in the cooking liquid, then remove the mushrooms with a slotted spoon.

2 Meanwhile, remove the soft centre and seeds from the cucumber pieces, using a sharp knife, potato peeler, apple corer or chopstick. Mix the crab with the spinach and season with salt, pepper and lemon juice. Stuff the cucumber pieces with the crab mixture. (Any left over will make delicious sandwiches.) Set aside.

3 Heat a little oil in a small frying pan and pour in half the egg mixture. Tilt the pan to coat the bottom evenly, then cook until a thick omelette is made. Remove from the pan and make a second omelette in the same way.

4 Lay the omelettes on a work surface, overlapping them a little to make a figure 8. Cover with the blanched lettuce leaves, tearing the lettuce to fit if necessary. Starting at one narrow end, roll up the omelette into a tight sausage. Cut across into 18 equal slices. Set aside.

5 To serve, on each plate arrange 1 prawn (or several smaller ones), 1 crab-stuffed cucumber piece, 3 slices of omelette roll and some mushrooms arranged on a square of lettuce.

Chicken porcupine balls and sesame beef balls with okra

The chicken porcupine balls
1 rasher streaky bacon, rind
  removed and roughly chopped
225 g/8 oz boned chicken breast,
  roughly chopped
1 medium onion, peeled and
  chopped
75 g/3 oz water chestnuts (tinned),
  roughly chopped
1 clove garlic, peeled and crushed
2.5-cm/1-inch cube root ginger,
  peeled and chopped
salt and pepper
225 g/8 oz pudding rice, soaked in
  cold water for 1 hour, drained and
  dried on kitchen paper

The sesame beef balls
350 g/12 oz lean steak, chopped
40 g/1½ oz streaky bacon, rind
  removed and roughly chopped
15 ml/1 tbsp cornflour
15 ml/1 tbsp chopped celery
15 ml/1 tbsp chopped carrot
15 ml/1 tbsp chopped mushroom
2 spring onions, chopped
25 ml/5 tsp soy sauce
10 ml/2 tsp dry sherry
2.5 ml/½ tsp salt
pepper

1 egg, beaten
oil for deep frying
30 ml/2 tbsp bottled hoisin sauce
10 ml/2 tsp sugar
15 ml/1 tbsp white sesame seeds

To serve
225 g/8 oz okra
bottled sweet chilli sauce
bottled hoisin or Chinese plum
  sauce

1 To make the chicken porcupine balls, place the bacon, chopped chicken breast, onion, water chestnuts, garlic and ginger in the container of a blender or food processor. Season with salt and pepper to taste and blend until a smooth paste forms. With dampened hands, form the mixture into walnut-sized balls, then roll in the rice until coated. Place the balls in a steamer, allowing a 1-cm/½-inch space between each. Set aside.
2 To make the beef balls, place the steak, bacon, cornflour, chopped vegetables, 10 ml/ 2 tsp of the soy sauce, the sherry, and salt and pepper to taste in the container of the blender or food processor and process until just amalgamated. Do not overprocess. With floured hands, form into walnut-sized balls. Coat in beaten egg.
3 Place the steamer containing the chicken balls over boiling water and steam for 20 minutes.
4 Meanwhile, heat the oil for deep frying to fairly hot and deep fry the beef balls until well browned. Drain on kitchen paper and set aside. Remove all but 30 ml/2 tbsp oil from the pan and add the hoisin sauce, the remaining soy sauce, the sugar and sesame seeds. Heat the pan, shaking occasionally, and add the beef balls and cook until they are coated with the sauce and deeply coloured.
5 Meanwhile, remove the little stalk ends from the okra and steam for 10 minutes.
6 To serve, divide the beef balls and the chicken porcupine balls between 6 plates and garnish with the okra. Add a little pool of each sauce to the plates, or serve the sauces separately in little individual dishes. If liked, eat with chopsticks.

Oranges in green ginger wine

6 large oranges (or more)
green ginger wine

1 Peel the oranges, removing all the white pith, and slice across the segments as thinly as possible. Lay the segments in the bottom of a pretty serving dish.
2 Pour over enough ginger wine almost to cover. Cover the bowl with plastic wrap and leave to macerate overnight or for several hours in the refrigerator.
3 To serve, spoon onto chilled plates.

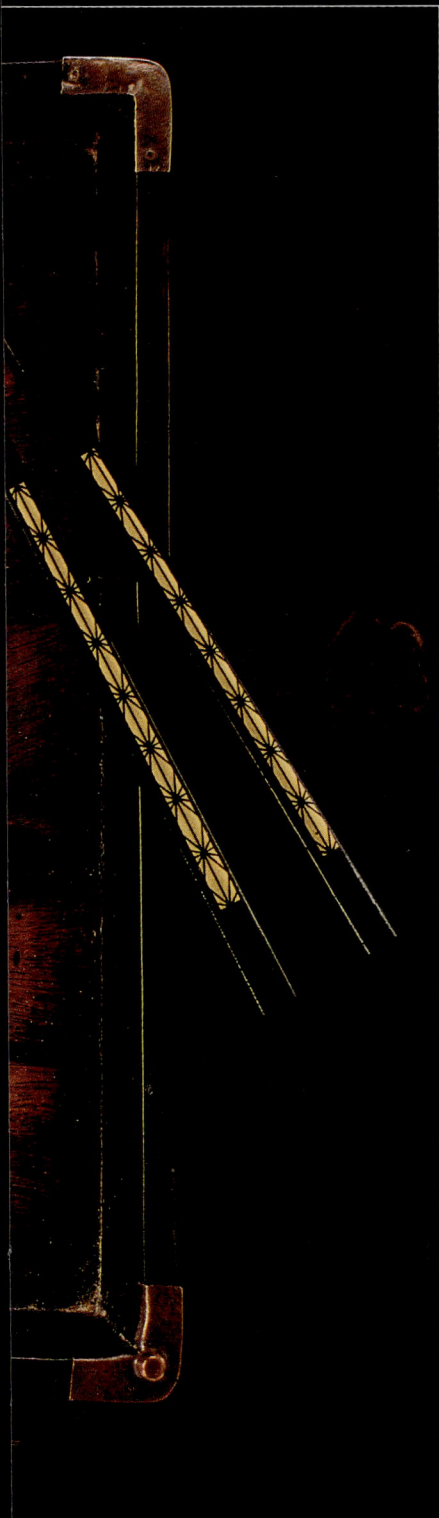

Left: Oriental hors d'oeuvre
Above: Chicken porcupine balls and sesame beef balls with okra
Below: Oranges in green ginger wine

Palm heart, avocado and Parmesan salad

•

Chillied prawns in pineapples with celery, grapes and toasted almonds

•

Guava jelly with orange and white rum sauce

Palm heart, avocado and Parmesan salad

1 (400 g/14 oz) tin palm hearts,
    drained
1 large or 2 small ripe avocado
    pears
juice of 1 lemon
75 g/3 oz piece of Parmesan
    cheese
pepper
walnut or olive oil

1 Cut the palm hearts into small bite-size sticks.
2 Peel the avocados, cut in half and remove the stones. Cut the flesh into thick slices lengthways and toss in lemon juice until each piece is coated.
3 Using a potato peeler, pare the Parmesan into long curling slivers. (This should not be done until the last minute or the cheese will go dry.)

4 Carefully fold the palm hearts and avocado slices together, so as not to break the slices. Divide between 6 bowls or plates and arrange the cheese shavings on top. Sprinkle with pepper to taste and drizzle with the oil.
Note: This salad does not need salt as there is sufficient in the cheese.

Chillied prawns in pineapples with celery, grapes and toasted almonds

3 small ripe pineapples
15 ml/1 tbsp vegetable oil
1 medium onion, peeled and
chopped
1 clove garlic, peeled and crushed
2 large sticks celery, coarsely
chopped
15 ml/1 tbsp chopped red or green
pepper
10 ml/2 tsp chilli powder
salt and pepper
300 ml/½ pint chicken stock
(see page 19)

20 ml/4 tsp arrowroot, dissolved
in a little water
450 g/1 lb peeled cooked prawns,
thawed if frozen
225 g/8 oz small green seedless
grapes
75 g/3 oz blanched, split almonds,
toasted (see page 25)
6 large or 12 small prawns in
shells

1 Cut the pineapples in half lengthways, through the crown of green leaves. Being careful not to cut through the skin, remove all the flesh. Set the shells aside. Cut the flesh into bite-sized pieces, discarding the hard core, and set aside.
2 Heat the oil in a large saucepan and cook the onion until transparent. Add the garlic, celery, red or green pepper and chilli powder. Add salt and pepper to taste. Stir fry for 2-3 minutes. Stir in the stock. Bring to the boil and simmer for 15 minutes. Thicken with the arrowroot, stirring well.
3 Add the peeled prawns, grapes and pineapple pieces and continue to cook gently until just heated through. The prawns will toughen if cooked for too long.
4 To serve, pile the cooked prawn mixture into the pineapple half shells and garnish with toasted almonds and prawns in shells.

Guava jelly with orange and white rum sauce

1 (400 g/14 oz) tin guavas in syrup
generous 10 ml/2 tsp powdered
gelatine
2 large oranges, peeled and pips
removed
30 ml/2 tbsp white rum, or to
taste

1 Drain the syrup from the guavas, measure it and place in a bowl. Dissolve half the gelatine in enough water to make the syrup up to 300 ml/½ pint, following the instructions on the packet. Mix with the syrup and divide the mixture between 6 individual dampened moulds or 1 large one (600 ml/1 pint). Chill until set.
2 Meanwhile, purée the guavas in a blender or food processor and strain through a sieve. Dissolve the rest of the gelatine in sufficient water to make the fruit purée up to 300 ml/ ½ pint. Mix with the purée, then pour this mixture equally over the jellied syrup mixture in the moulds to make a separate layer. Return to the refrigerator and chill until completely set.
3 To make the sauce, place the oranges and rum in the container of a blender or food processor and blend until smooth. Strain through a sieve.
4 To serve, dip the moulds very briefly in hot water and turn out onto chilled plates. Surround with the sauce.
Note: These jellies look equally pretty made in small wine glasses with the sauce poured on the top.

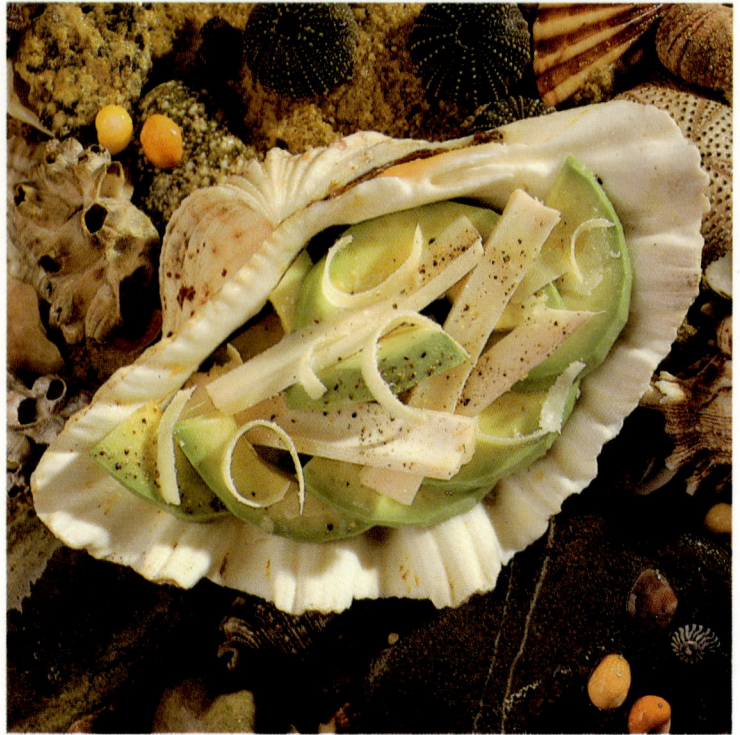

Above: Palm heart, avocado and Parmesan salad
Left: Chillied prawns in pineapples with celery, grapes and toasted almonds
Below: Guava jelly with orange and white rum sauce

Above: Gado gado salad
Left: Spiced crab with bacon-wrapped water chestnuts
Below: Tropical fruit kebabs

Gado gado salad

•

Spiced crab with bacon-wrapped water chestnuts

•

Tropical fruit kebabs

Gado gado salad

450 g/1 lb cabbage, shredded,
*   blanched and refreshed*
*   (see page 25)*
450 g/1 lb bean sprouts, blanched
*   and refreshed*
225 g/8 oz green beans, trimmed,
*   blanched and refreshed*
½ cucumber, sliced as thinly as
*   possible*
3 eggs, hard-boiled, shelled and
*   roughly chopped*

The sauce
15 ml/1 tbsp vegetable oil

1 medium onion, peeled and chopped
1 clove garlic, peeled and crushed
10 ml/2 tsp chilli powder
grated rind of ½ lemon
15 ml/1 tbsp lemon juice
10 ml/2 tsp brown sugar
5 ml/1 tsp soy sauce
5 ml/1 tsp salt
175 g/6 fl oz coconut milk
*   (see page 20)*
60 ml/4 tbsp peanut butter
120 ml/4 fl oz water

1 Heat the oil in a saucepan and cook the onion and garlic until transparent. Add the rest of the sauce ingredients. Simmer gently for 15 minutes, stirring constantly with a wooden spoon and making sure the peanut butter is dissolved. Cool.

2 To serve, arrange the cabbage, bean sprouts, beans, cucumber and eggs on 6 plates or bowls and spoon over the sauce.

Spiced crab with bacon-wrapped water chestnuts

6 small dressed crabs in shells
30 ml/2 tbsp plain yogurt
salt and pepper
1.25-2.5 ml/¼-½ tsp Chinese
  five-spice powder, or to taste
juice of 1 lemon
15 ml/1 tbsp snipped fresh chives
6 rashers streaky bacon, rinds
  removed
18 water chestnuts, tinned

1 Remove all the crab meat from the shells and mix with the yogurt. Season with salt and pepper, five-spice powder and lemon juice. Replace the mixture neatly in the shells. Sprinkle with the chives. Set aside.
2 Stretch the bacon rashers with the back of a knife and cut each crossways into 3 equal portions. Wrap each water chestnut in a piece of bacon and secure with ½ wooden cocktail stick. Cook under a preheated hot grill until the bacon is crisp, turning once.
3 To serve, place 3 hot bacon and water chestnut rolls on each filled crab and serve immediately.

Tropical fruit kebabs

1 small pineapple, peeled, cored and
  cut into bite-size pieces
1 large banana, peeled and cut into
  bite-size pieces
1 small wedge of water melon,
  peeled and cut into bite-size pieces
1 large or 2 small mangoes, peeled,
  stoned and cut into bite-size
  pieces
1 medium papaya, peeled, deseeded
  and cut into bite-size pieces
2 kiwi fruit, peeled and cut into bite-
  size pieces
juice of 2 large lemons

1 Toss the fruit pieces in lemon juice to stop discoloration.
2 Just before serving thread the fruit attractively onto wooden or metal kebab skewers.
3 These quantities are approximate and other exotic fruit can be substituted for those not available.
Note: If desired, serve with lightly whipped cream laced with rum.

Left: Deep fried tofu with steamed beansprouts and chillied peanut sauce
Below: Toffee cherries

Above: Spice island beef and carrots with black mustard seed

Deep-fried tofu with steamed beansprouts and chillied peanut sauce

●

Spice island beef and carrots with black mustard seed

●

Toffee cherries

Deep-fried tofu with steamed beansprouts and chillied peanut sauce

400 g/14 oz firm tofu (see page 36)
15 ml/1 tbsp vegetable oil
1 small onion, peeled and chopped
2 cloves garlic, peeled and
*   crushed*
2-cm/¾-inch cube root ginger,
*   peeled and finely chopped*
2.5 ml/½ tsp salt

5 ml/1 tsp chilli powder, or more to
*   taste*
300 ml/½ pint water
45 ml/3 tbsp peanut butter
*   (smooth or crunchy)*
700 g/1½ lb bean sprouts
oil for deep frying
30 ml/6 tsp soy sauce

1 Wrap the tofu in a double thickness of kitchen paper and place a flat weight on top (such as a small loaf tin half full of water). Leave to press and drain for 1 hour. Cut into 2-cm/¾-inch cubes.
2 Heat the vegetable oil in a small saucepan and cook the onion until transparent. Add the garlic and ginger and cook for 2 more minutes. Stir in the salt, chilli powder and water and simmer for 5 minutes. Place this mixture with the peanut butter in the container of a blender or food processor and blend until smooth. Return to the saucepan and leave to reheat gently.
3 Meanwhile, steam the beansprouts until just hot. Drain. Deep fry the tofu cubes until golden and crispy, turning once. Drain.
4 To serve, divide the bean sprouts between 6 heated bowls or plates and top with the tofu and sauce. Drizzle a teaspoon of the soy sauce over each serving.
Note: Served with rice, this dish makes a delicious main course.

Spice island beef and carrots with black mustard seed

15 ml/1 tbsp vegetable oil
900 g/2 lb piece of rolled topside
or brisket of beef
30 ml/2 tbsp soy sauce
60 ml/4 tbsp dry white wine
2 cloves garlic, peeled and
crushed
1 star anise flower (see page 30)

15 ml/1 tbsp sugar
pepper
3 medium carrots, peeled and cut
into thin rounds
15 g/½ oz butter
7.5 ml/1½ tsp lemon juice
pinch of salt
5 ml/1 tsp black mustard seed

1 Heat the oil in a heavy pan just large enough to fit the piece of meat snugly. Brown the meat on all sides, then add the soy sauce, wine, garlic and star anise flower. Cover the pan tightly and leave to cook undisturbed over a very low heat for 1 hour.

2 Add the sugar and a generous amount of ground black pepper. Replace the lid and cook for a further hour.

3 Lift out the meat and allow to rest for a while. Boil over a fierce heat to reduce the liquid in the pan until a small amount of sticky sauce remains.

4 Meanwhile, steam the carrots until just cooked. Melt the butter in a small saucepan and when sizzling add the lemon juice, salt and mustard seed. Shake the pan until the seeds 'jump', then add the carrots and toss well. Keep hot.

5 Cut the meat into small fingers or cubes and toss in the sauce until coated.

6 To serve, place a portion of beef on each of 6 heated plates and then divide out the carrots. Serve with a side dish of plain boiled rice.

Note: Any remaining meat is delicious served cold.

Toffee cherries

225 g/8 oz granulated sugar
250 ml/8 fl oz water
about 50 cherries with stalks,
washed and dried

1 Place the sugar and water in a small heavy-bottomed saucepan and bring slowly to the boil, stirring to dissolve the sugar. Simmer over a gentle heat, without stirring, until the syrup turns a pale amber colour. Remove from the heat.

2 Working very quickly, dip the cherries in the syrup and place, stems up, on greaseproof paper. Leave until the caramel coating cools and hardens. (You may find that the 'toffee' will harden too quickly, so make two batches, preparing half the syrup each time.)

3 To serve, simply divide the cherries between 6 plates.

Note: It is advisable not to make this dish too far in advance as after a while the toffee coating loses its crispness and begins to turn sticky.

THE AUTUMN HARVEST

*The countryside dresses itself in a final blaze of glory
and this is the busiest time of the year for country
people. Crops must be quickly harvested and brought
in before the first frost. Fruit must be picked before it
falls to the ground. This is the time for preserving and
pickling, drying and smoking. Traditionally the
family pig was killed and cured to make bacon and
ham, sausages and black puddings.*

*The forests and hedgerows are full of wild foods for
anyone to pick – chestnuts and hazelnuts,
blackberries and mushrooms. Our squirrel ing
instincts urge us to 'put things by' for winter use.
City dwellers too can enjoy something of these
autumn pleasures, even if simply by converting some
windfall apples into a few pots of herb jelly, or by
freezing some wild blackberries gathered on a Sunday
afternoon forray into the country.*

*As the mornings become chilly and the evenings draw
in, we begin to long for warm, comforting and more
substantial food. Dishes based on traditional English
recipes and the simple rustic fare of other countries
make perfect eating for this time of year – warming
soups and casseroles, pies and puddings and cooked
fruity desserts.*

Beetroot and spinach salad with caraway-orange dressing and hot bacon
●
Beef in Guinness with horseradish dumplings
●
Pan-fried apples with butter, cream and walnuts

Beetroot and spinach salad with caraway-orange dressing and hot bacon

6 rashers streaky bacon (smoked
    preferably), rinds removed, cut
    across into 1-cm/½-inch strips
15 ml/2 tbsp olive oil
1 clove garlic, peeled and crushed
salt and pepper
5 ml/1 tsp sugar
generous 5 ml/1 tsp caraway seeds

juice of 1 orange
700 g/1½ lb cooked beetroot,
    peeled and diced
175 g/6 oz young spinach leaves,
    washed and dried
generous 15 ml/1 tbsp parsley,
    chopped

1 Slowly fry the bacon in the oil to let the fat run. When the bacon is crisp, remove with a slotted spoon and keep warm.
2 Add the garlic to the pan and cook for 1 minute. Add salt and pepper to taste, the sugar, caraway seeds, and orange juice and cook for 2 minutes more over a low heat, stirring all the ingredients and scraping any bits off the bottom of the pan into the dressing.

3 Just before serving, tip the beetroot into the pan and shake it around, so that it is coated with the dressing but not further cooked.
4 To serve, arrange the spinach leaves in 6 bowls or on 6 plates. Divide the dressed beetroot between these. Sprinkle with the hot bacon strips and the parsley and serve immediately.

Beef in Guinness with horseradish dumplings

seasoned flour
900 g/2 lb lean stewing beef,
    cubed
45 ml/3 tbsp vegetable oil
2 large onions, peeled and
    coarsely chopped
10 ml/2 tsp sugar
5 ml/1 tsp dry English mustard
15 ml/1 tbsp concentrated tomato
    purée
1 bay leaf
1 strip orange rind, about 2.5 x 7.5
    cm/1 x 3 inches
5 ml/1 tsp thyme (or half this
    amount of dried thyme)

salt and pepper
600 ml/1 pint Guinness
450 g/1 lb carrots, peeled and cut
    into sticks

The dumplings
50 g/2 oz fresh brown breadcrumbs
50 g/2 oz plain flour
50 g/2 oz shredded suet
2.5 ml/½ tsp baking powder
salt and pepper
1 egg, beaten
horseradish sauce or relish
    (bottled)

1 Place the seasoned flour in a large plastic bag and add the meat. Shake the bag until the cubes are coated with flour. Remove and shake off the excess flour. Heat 30 ml/2 tbsp of the oil in a heavy saucepan or flameproof casserole. Fry the meat in batches in the hot oil until sealed and browned on all sides. Remove with a slotted spoon and set aside.

2 Add the remaining spoonful of oil to the pan and fry the onions until well browned. Add the sugar, mustard, tomato purée, bay leaf, orange rind, thyme, salt and pepper to taste and the Guinness. Bring to the boil, stirring well. Return the meat to the pan. If the liquid does not quite cover the meat, top up with water. Cover and simmer over a low heat, or in a low oven, for 2-2½ hours or until the meat is tender.

3 About 30 minutes before serving, prepare the dumplings. Mix the dry ingredients and season to taste. Bind with the egg to make a firm dough. Roll into a rough sausage shape on a floured work surface and divide into 6 equal portions. With floured hands roll each portion into a ball. Poke a hole into the side of each ball. Into the hole put a little horseradish sauce or relish. Close the hole and seal well.

4 About 20 minutes before serving, cook the dumplings in gently simmering salted water or stock. Steam the carrots until tender but still crisp. Stir the carrots into the beef mixture.

5 To serve, spoon portions of the casserole on to 6 hot plates. Top each serving with a dumpling.

Pan-fried apples with butter, cream and walnuts

6 Cox's apples (or other dessert
   apples), peeled, cored and sliced
juice of 1 lemon
75 g/3 oz unsalted butter
45 ml/3 tbsp sugar
150 ml/¼ pint single cream
50 g/2 oz shelled walnut halves

1 Toss the apple slices in the lemon juice to prevent them discolouring.

2 Heat the butter in a frying pan on a very low heat. Do not let the butter brown. Add the apples to the pan with the sugar and cook very gently, turning once, until the apples just begin to soften and are heated through. Do not overcook.

3 Add the cream and nuts. Continue to cook only until the cream is hot, stirring to amalgamate the sauce but being particularly careful not to break the apple slices.

4 To serve, divide between 6 heated plates or bowls.

Above: Beetroot and spinach salad with caraway-orange dressing and hot bacon
Opposite page: Beef in Guinness with horseradish dumplings
Right: Pan-fried apples with butter, cream and walnuts

Tomato soup with vodka

•

Black pudding with fried apples and mustard cream sauce

•

Rum plum pie with vanilla custard

Tomato soup with vodka

1.8 litres/3 pints chicken stock
   (see page 19)
1 small onion, peeled and chopped
1 clove garlic, peeled and crushed
700 g/1½ lb ripe tomatoes,
   quartered
5 ml/1 tsp sugar
pinch of dried marjoram or
   oregano, or 15 ml/1 tbsp
   chopped, fresh basil if available

salt and pepper
Worcestershire sauce
Tabasco sauce
45 ml/3 tbsp vodka, or more if
   liked

1 Bring the stock to the boil in a saucepan. Add the onion and garlic and simmer for 5 minutes. Add the tomatoes, sugar and herbs and season to taste with salt and pepper. Simmer for 5 minutes more. Do not cook longer as the 'fresh' taste of the tomatoes will be lost.

2 Pour into a blender or food processor and blend until smooth. Pour through a metal sieve to strain out any skin or seeds, then return to the pan.

3 Add a dash of Worcestershire sauce, but not too much. Add a dash of Tabasco, again only just enough to give a 'bite' to the soup. Reheat. Just before serving add the vodka.

4 To serve, pour into heated bowls.

Black pudding with fried apples and mustard cream sauce

30 ml/2 tbsp vegetable oil
900 g/2 lb black pudding, cut into
1-cm/½-inch slices diagonally
50 g/2 oz butter
2 firm eating apples, cored and
sliced

1 small onion, peeled and chopped
300 ml/½ pint double cream
10 ml/2 tsp dry English mustard
salt and pepper
freshly cooked seasonal vegetable

1 Heat the oil in a frying pan and fry the slices of black pudding over a moderate heat for 2-3 minutes each side. Remove from the pan with a slotted spoon and keep warm.
2 Add the butter to the pan and fry the apple slices over a low heat until just beginning to soften. Remove from the pan with a slotted spoon and keep warm.
3 Add the onion to the pan and cook over a fairly high heat until softened and transparent. Add the cream, mustard and salt and pepper to taste. Cook over a moderate heat, stirring constantly and scraping all the bits from the bottom of the pan into the sauce. Allow to bubble for 2-3 minutes.
4 To serve, arrange alternate slices of black pudding and apples on heated plates. Pour over the sauce and add the vegetable.

Rum plum pie with vanilla custard

6 (9-cm/3½-inch) discs cut from
thinly rolled puff pastry
(see pages 21/22)
900 g/2 lb plums, halved and
stoned
45 ml/3 tbsp soft dark brown
sugar
45 ml/3 tbsp dark rum

The custard
600 ml/1 pint milk
2 egg yolks
generous 15 ml/1 tbsp cornflour
15 ml/1 tbsp sugar
2.5 ml/½ tsp vanilla essence

1 Bake the pastry discs on a greased baking sheet in a preheated 220°C/425°F/Gas 7 oven for 15 minutes or until puffed and golden. With a knife, split each pastry disc into two as you would cut a scone. Set aside and keep warm.
2 Place the plums in a saucepan with the brown sugar and rum. Cover and cook over a gentle heat until the plums are softened but not mushy. The cooking time will depend on the ripeness and variety of the plums.
3 Meanwhile, make the custard. Bring the milk almost to boiling point in a saucepan. While this is heating whisk the egg yolks with the cornflour, sugar and vanilla essence until pale. When the milk is almost boiling, pour it in a steady stream onto the egg mixture, whisking all the time. Strain through a sieve back into the saucepan. Cook over the lowest possible heat until thickened. This custard will not go lumpy if stirred all the time it is cooking.
4 To serve, place a pastry 'bottom' on each plate and spoon over the plums. Add the pastry 'lids'. Spoon some custard to the side of the plate.
Note: This is equally good served hot or cold.

Above: Tomato soup with vodka
Left: Black pudding with fried apples and mustard cream sauce
Below: Rum plum pie with vanilla custard

Fried stuffed mushrooms in batter

●

Orange oxtail with pumpkin

●

Chestnut creams

Fried stuffed mushrooms in batter

1 small onion, peeled and finely
  chopped
2 cloves garlic, peeled and
  crushed
25 g/1 oz softened butter
15 ml/1 tbsp chopped parsley
50 g/2 oz dry-roasted peanuts,
  roughly chopped
50 g/2 oz softened cream cheese
salt and pepper
450 g/1 lb small mushrooms,
  stems removed and reserved for
  another use
oil for deep frying

The batter
175 g/6 oz plain flower
10 ml/2 tsp bicarbonate of soda
175 g/6 fl oz water
salt and pepper
10 ml/2 tsp lemon juice or vinegar

1 Mix the onion, garlic, butter, parsley, peanuts and cream cheese together and season with salt and pepper to taste. Stuff the mushrooms caps with the mixture. With a knife, smooth the stuffing level with the edges of the mushrooms. Set aside.
2 Make the batter (but not too far in advance). Mix the flour with the bicarbonate of soda and water and season generously with salt and pepper. Beat until smooth. Just before using, beat in the lemon juice or vinegar.
3 Dip the stuffed mushrooms in the batter and deep dry in very hot oil until batter is deep golden and crisp. Do not overcrowd the pan, but fry in batches. Drain on crumpled kitchen paper. To keep each batch warm, place uncovered in a warm oven.
4 Serve immediately.
Note: These are delicious handed round at a drinks party.

Orange oxtail with pumpkin

30 ml/2 tbsp olive oil
2 large onions, peeled and
    coarsely chopped
1.3-1.8 kg/3-4 lb oxtail, cut into
    thick sections
2 cloves garlic, peeled and
    crushed
finely grated rind and juice of
    1 small orange
2 bay leaves
2.5 ml/½ tsp juniper berries,
    crushed

100 g/4 oz mushrooms, sliced
7.5 ml/1½ tsp redcurrant jelly
small dash of Worcestershire
    sauce
salt and pepper
900 g/2 lb pumpkin, peeled and
    cut into bite-size cubes
2 large oranges, peeled and
    divided into segments

1 Heat the oil in a large saucepan or flame-proof casserole and fry the onions until golden. Add the oxtail, garlic, orange rind and juice, bay leaves and juniper berries. Pour over enough cold water just to cover. Bring to the boil, then cover and cook over a gentle heat or in a low oven for 3 hours.
2 Remove the oxtail and put in a covered bowl. Pour the sauce into another bowl. Leave both bowls in the refrigerator overnight or for several hours.
3 Remove the hardened fat from the top of the sauce and discard. Return the sauce and the oxtail to the pan and reheat. Add the mush-rooms, redcurrant jelly and Worcestershire sauce, and season with salt and pepper to taste. Simmer for 15-20 minutes.
4 Meanwhile, steam the pumpkin sprinkled with a little salt for about 15 minutes or until tender.
5 Just before serving, add the orange segments to the oxtail and allow to warm through for a couple of minutes.
6 To serve, divide the meat and sauce between 6 heated plates with the pumpkin. Bread will be welcomed to mop up the sauce.
Note: If pumpkin is not available, serve steamed swede.

Chestnut creams

1 (435 g/15½ oz) tin chestnut
    purée with glucose
15 ml/1 tbsp sugar
grated rind and juice of ½ small
    lemon
5 ml/1 tsp ground ginger
generous 45 ml/3 tbsp brandy

45 ml/3 tbsp cream
300 ml/½ pint double cream,
    whipped until stiff
julienne strips of lemon rind,
    blanched and drained (see page
    25)
30 ml/2 tbsp clear honey

1 Place the chestnut purée, sugar, lemon rind and juice, ginger, brandy, and unwhipped cream in the container of a blender or food processor. Blend until well amalgamated, then remove to a bowl and fold in the whipped cream.
2 Spoon into 6 glasses or dishes and chill for at least 2 hours.
3 To serve, sprinkle with lemon julienne strips and pour 5 ml/1 tsp honey over each serving.

Above: Fried stuffed mushrooms in batter
Left: Orange oxtail with pumpkin
Below: Chestnut creams

Above left: Sweet potato soup with garlic croûtons
Left: Shellfish puddings
Above: Pears poached in white Lambrusco

Sweet potato soup with garlic croûtons
●
Shellfish puddings
●
Pears poached in white Lambrusco

Sweet potato soup with garlic croûtons

45 ml/3 tbsp vegetable oil
2 rashers smoked, streaky bacon,
   rinds removed, chopped
1 large onion, peeled and chopped
450 g/1 lb sweet potatoes, peeled
   and cut into cubes
5 ml/1 tsp chopped sage, or
   2.5 ml/½ tsp dried sage

5 ml/1 tsp turmeric
1.5 litres/2½ pints chicken stock
   (see page 19)
salt and pepper
2 cloves garlic, peeled and crushed
3 slices white bread, crusts
   removed, cut into small cubes

1 Heat 15 ml/1 tbsp oil in a heavy saucepan and fry the bacon pieces slowly until the fat runs out. Add the onion and continue to cook over a medium heat until the onion is transparent. Add the sweet potato and cook for a further 3-4 minutes, stirring constantly. Add the sage, turmeric, stock, and salt and pepper to taste. Bring to the boil, then cover and simmer over a gentle heat for 25 minutes.

2 Pour into the container of a blender or food processor and blend until smooth. Return to the pan and reheat.
3 To make the croûtons, heat the remaining oil in a frying pan and add the garlic and the cubes of bread. Fry gently, turning once, until the croûtons are crisp and golden.
4 To serve, pour the soup into 6 heated bowls and scatter on the croûtons.

Shellfish puddings

25 g/1 oz butter
1 small onion, peeled and chopped
1 small stick celery, finely
   chopped
18 mussels, steamed, opened and
   shells discarded (see page 26)
225 g/8 oz cooked, peeled prawns
   (thawed if frozen)
225 g/8 oz cockles, cooked and
   shelled (see page 30)
100 g/4 oz sweetcorn kernels
   (tinned or frozen)

300 ml/½ pint milk
2 (43 g/1½ oz) tins dressed crab
salt and pepper
freshly cooked seasonal vegetable
   tossed in butter

The pastry
450 g/1 lb self-raising flour
225 g/8 oz shredded suet
15 ml/1 tbsp chopped parsley
salt and pepper
250 ml/8 fl oz water

1 Melt the butter in a small saucepan and cook the onion and celery over a gentle heat until the onion is transparent. Remove to a bowl and add the mussels, prawns, cockles and sweetcorn.

2 Thoroughly mix in a jug the milk and crab meat and season to tast with salt and pepper.
3 Make the suet pastry: mix the flour, suet and parsley in a bowl and season generously with salt and pepper. Add the water and mix

with a fork to form a dough. Gather together with flour hands, and on a floured work surface form into a rough sausage shape. Divide this into 6 equal portions. Roll out each portion to a rough circle about 5-mm/¼-inch thick. Cut one-third of the circle away in a wedge shape, and reserve. Grease 6 individual pudding bowls and, using the large segments of pastry, carefully line them, pushing the dough well down into the corners (see page 26).

4 Divide the mussel mixture between these but do not allow the fish to come more than two-thirds of the way up the pastry. Pour some of the crab and milk mixture onto the fish, just to cover. Cut small circles from the remaining segments of pastry just to fit inside the bowls. Place these over the filling and bring over the pastry 'walls', pinching them onto the lids to seal. There should be a small space at the top of the bowl to allow the pudding to rise. Cover each bowl tightly with a small circle of greased foil.

5 Steam over boiling water for 1½ hours.

6 To serve, turn out the puddings onto heated plates. Place the vegetable alongside the puddings. Serve immediately.

Pears poached in white Lambrusco

6 hard pears, peeled but with the
stalks left on
30 ml/2 tbsp sugar
400 ml/14 fl oz white Lambrusco
or other sweet white wine
5 ml/1 tsp arrowroot, dissolved in
a little water

1 Place the pears in a pan just big enough to fit them snugly in one layer, stalks up. Sprinkle over the sugar and pour over the wine. Bring to the boil, then cover and simmer gently until the pears are tender and look a little transparent. This could take up to 1½ hours, depending on the type of pear. Do not overcook, as the pears must retain their shape.

2 Remove the pears and set aside to cool. Boil to reduce the cooking liquid over a fierce heat until only 300 ml/½ pint remains, then thicken with the arrowroot, stirring well. Chill the sauce and pears separately.

3 To serve, slice a fraction off the bottom of each pear to give it a flat base. Stand each on a plate or in a bowl and pour over the sauce. This does not really need cream.

Note: If you have the time and patience, before cooking the pears remove the cores from the underneath using a potato peeler, apple corer or sharp knife.

Above: Red vegetable broth with onion bread

Above: Chicken and cabbage pie
Right: Cherry berry compôte

Red vegetable broth with onion bread

●

Chicken and cabbage pie

●

Cherry berry compôte

Red vegetable broth with onion bread

1.8 litres/3 pints chicken stock
*   (see page 19)*
generous 45 ml/3 tbsp diced
*   cooked beetroot*
generous 45 ml/3 tbsp diced red
*   pepper*
generous 45 ml/3 tbsp peeled,
*   seeded, and diced tomato*
salt and pepper

For the breads
30 ml/2 tbsp vegetable oil

450 g/1 lb onions, peeled and
*   finely chopped*
1 (14 g/½ oz) packet 'fast action'
*   dried yeast (see page 34)*
700 g/1½ lb strong white bread
*   flour*
10 ml/2 tsp salt
25 g/1 oz lard
450 ml/¾ pint milk, heated to
*   blood temperature*
1 egg yolk mixed with
*   15 ml/1 tbsp milk*

1 First make the onion bread. Heat the oil in a frying pan and fry the onions until brown but not burned. Remove to a bowl and allow to cool.

2 Mix the yeast with the flour and salt in a large bowl. Rub in the lard. Stir in the milk and mix to form a dough. Knead for 10 minutes. Roll into a long sausage, or several smaller sausages if this is easier to handle. Divide into 12 equal pieces.

3 Roll out each piece of dough to form a circle about 15 cm/6 inches in diameter. Place a mound of onion in the centre of each dough circle. Dampen the edges of the dough and fold over to make half-moon-shaped pasties or turnovers. Press the edges to seal.

4 Place on a baking sheet, leaving space between each for expansion. Leave to rise in a warm place until almost doubled in size, 1-2 hours.

5 Brush the breads with the egg yolk and milk mixture to glaze. Bake in a preheated 230°C/450°F/Gas 8 oven for about 20 minutes or until cooked and golden.

6 Meanwhile, bring the stock to the boil in a large saucepan and add the beetroot and red pepper. Simmer for 5 minutes. Add the tomato and simmer for a further 5 minutes only. Add more seasoning if necessary.

7 To serve, spoon the soup into 6 heated bowls, making sure everyone gets a good share of the vegetables. Serve the onion breads on separate plates. These do not need butter and are best served straight from the oven.

Note: The quantities for the dough make 12 quite large breads. One per person is enough to serve with this meal. The remainder can be frozen or reheated for breakfast next morning.

Chicken and cabbage pie

75 g/3 oz butter
1 medium onion, peeled and
chopped
225 g/8 oz green or white
cabbage, cored and finely
shredded
salt and pepper
100 g/4 oz mushrooms, sliced
cream cheese pastry made with
175 g/6 oz flour (see page 21)

100 g/4 oz softened cream cheese
chopped fresh or dried herbs – basil,
marjoram, thyme or tarragon
(select one variety to taste)
350 g/12 oz cooked chicken meat
(see page 31), sliced or chopped
1 bunch watercress, washed,
picked over and drained

1 Melt 40 g/1½ oz of the butter in a saucepan and cook the onion and cabbage, covered, until the onion is transparent and the cabbage has wilted. Season to taste with salt and pepper.
2 Heat the remaining butter in a frying pan and cook the mushrooms until softened. Season to taste with salt and black pepper.
3 Roll out half the pastry and use to line a 25-cm/10-inch ovenproof plate, or shallow pie dish. Spread the cream cheese over the bottom of the pastry, to within 2.5 cm/1 inch of the edge of the plate. Sprinkle with the herbs. Spread over the cabbage and onion mixture, then cover with the chicken, and place the mushrooms on top. Roll out the rest of the pastry and cover the top of the pie. Seal the edges with water. Cut suitable decorations for the top from the pastry trimmings and make a decorative edge. Brush with a little milk to glaze.
4 Bake in a preheated 200°C/400°F/Gas 6 oven for 15 minutes, then turn the oven down to 180°C/350°F/Gas 4 and continue to bake for a further 20-25 minutes or until the pastry is crisp and golden.
5 To serve, cut the pie into wedges and place on hot plates with a little watercress.

Cherry berry compôte

450 g/1 lb fresh red cherries,
stoned (if unavailable use tinned
black cherries)
450 g/1 lb blackberries (if fresh
are unavailable use frozen)
45 ml/3 tbsp sugar
45 ml/3 tbsp brandy

1 Place all the ingredients in a heavy-bottomed saucepan. Cover and cook on a medium heat for 5 minutes.

2 To serve, spoon into 6 warmed bowls.
Note: Serve either hot or chilled, either way is equally delicious.

WINTER WARMTH
AND CELEBRATION

Winter approaches almost unnoticed as our thoughts are filled with the excitement of the coming seasonal festivities. The cold weather and long dark evenings, however, give us extra time to spend in the kitchen preparing more sophisticated and elegant meals. This is the time of year when little excuse is needed for giving parties and for spending that little extra on luxury ingredients.

Here are five carefully planned festive menus which, although satisfying the cravings for all the seasonal flavours, are so arranged that every one will feel satisfied but no one will feel uncomfortably overfed. These more unashamedly extravagant menus call for elegant settings, and now is the time for polishing the silver and ironing the lace cloth.

Clear chicken soup with peanut dumplings
●
Roasted duck with chestnut sauce, stewed blackberries and braised chicory
●
Hazelnut creams with apricot sauce

Clear chicken soup with peanut dumplings

*1.5 litres/2½ pints chicken stock
(see page 19)*

The dumplings
*50 g/2 oz fresh wholemeal
breadcrumbs
50 g/2 oz plain flour
50 g/2 oz shredded suet*

*50 g/2 oz dry-roasted peanuts,
coarsley chopped
2.5 ml/½ tsp baking powder
15 ml/1 tbsp finely chopped
parsley
salt and pepper
1 egg, beaten*

1 First make the dumplings. Place the bread-crumbs, flour, suet, peanuts, baking powder, and parsley in a mixing bowl. Mix well together. Add salt and pepper to taste. Stir in the egg to make a fairly stiff dough.
2 Turn the dough onto a floured work surface and with lightly floured hands form into 18 small balls.

3 Bring the broth to the boil in a large sauce-pan. Add the dumplings and simmer gently for 15 minutes.
4 To serve, divide the dumplings and soup between 6 heated bowls.

Roasted duck with chestnut sauce, stewed blackberries and braised chicory

*2 medium ducks
30 ml/2 tbsp clear honey
30 ml/2 tbsp lemon juice
40 g/1½ oz frozen blackberries
juice of 1 orange*

The vegetable
*6 heads chicory, about 700 g/1½ lb
juice of 1 lemon
7.5 ml/1½ tsp sugar
salt and pepper
50 g/2 oz butter, cut into small
pieces*

The sauce
*30 ml/2 tbsp brandy
600 ml/1 pint duck stock (made
from the giblets) or chicken stock
(see page 19)
grated rind of 1 orange
150 ml/¼ pint single cream
150 g/5 oz tinned unsweetened
chestnut purée*

1 About 24 hours in advance, pour a kettle of boiling water over each duck. This will tighten the skin. Dry thoroughly inside and out with kitchen paper, then hang or place

the ducks on a wire tray in a draughty place to dry for 24 hours.
2 Prick the skin of the ducks all over with a darning needle (this will allow the fat to run

out). Heat the honey with the lemon juice in a small saucepan until amalgamated. Paint this mixture all over the ducks. Place the ducks, breast side up, on a rack in a large roasting tin. Roast near the top of a preheated 260°C/ 500°F/Gas 9 oven for 15 minutes.

3 Meanwhile, blanch the chicory in a large pan of boiling water for 3 minutes. Drain, refresh in cold water and gently pat dry with kitchen paper. Place the chicory in a casserole, pour over the lemon juice, sprinkle with the sugar and season to taste with salt and pepper. Dot with the butter cut into small pieces. Cover tightly.

4 Turn the oven down to 180°C/350°F/Gas 4. Place the chicory on a shelf underneath the ducks. Continue to roast the ducks without basting for a further 1 hour 10 minutes.

5 Meanwhile, stew the blackberries in the orange juice until just tender. Drain, and add the juice to the stock. Reserve the berries.

6 Remove the ducks from the roasting tin and keep warm. Pour off the fat from the roasting tin and reserve for future use. Place the roasting tin over a medium heat on top of the stove. Pour in the brandy and flame. Add the stock and fruit juice mixture and the grated orange rind and boil furiously until reduced to 300 ml/½ pint. Add the cream and continue to cook over a medium heat for 5 minutes. Do not boil.

7 Strain the sauce into the container of a blender or food processor. Add the chestnut purée and blend until smooth. Return to a saucepan and reheat. Check seasoning.

8 To serve, carve the ducks and arrange the pieces neatly on 6 heated plates. Allow each serving an equal share of the breast and the crispy skin. Place a braised chicory head and a few blackberries on each plate. Pour a little sauce over the meat.

Hazelnut creams with apricot sauce

50 g/2 oz hazelnuts
450 ml/¾ pint milk
3 egg yolks
40 g/1½ oz caster sugar
15 g/½ oz powdered gelatine
45 ml/3 tbsp water

30 ml/2 tbsp double cream,
*   whipped until stiff*

The sauce
100 g/4 oz dried apricots
300 ml/½ pint water

1 First make the sauce. Soak the dried apricots in the water for 4-6 hours.

2 Place the apricots and the water in a saucepan and stew until completely soft. Pour into the container of a food processor or blender and blend until smooth. Chill until required.

3 Toast the hazelnuts under a preheated grill until evenly browned. Grind to a powder and place in a saucepan with the milk. Bring gently to the boil and simmer for 5 minutes.

4 Cream the egg yolks and sugar together until pale and thick. Pour on the boiling milk

mixture, stirring well. Return to the pan and thicken over a low heat, stirring constantly. Do not allow to boil. Strain into a bowl and allow to cool.

5 Dissolve the gelatine in the water over a gentle heat and add to the cooled custard mixture. Stir well. Chill the mixture until it begins to thicken, then gently fold in the whipped cream. Pour immediately into 6 lightly oiled individual moulds. Chill until set.

6 To serve, turn out the creams onto 6 plates and surround with the apricot sauce.

Left: Clear chicken soup with peanut dumplings
Bottom: Roasted duck with chestnut sauce, stewed blackberries and braised chicory
Below: Hazelnut creams with apricot sauce

Above: Steamed celery in hazelnut sauce
Above right: Breast of pheasant with honey, lemon and caper sauce and chillied parsnip purée
Right: Chocolate and orange tofu mousse

Steamed celery in hazelnut sauce

●

Breast of pheasant with honey, lemon and caper sauce and chillied parsnip purée

●

Chocolate and orange tofu mousse

Steamed celery in hazelnut sauce

600 ml/1 pint milk
1 medium onion, peeled and
*   halved*
1 clove garlic, peeled and crushed
150 g/5 oz hazelnuts

150 g/5 oz white breadcrumbs
salt and pepper
2 heads of celery (about 550 g/1¼
*   lb), trimmed*
25 g/1 oz butter, cut into small
*   pieces*

1 Bring the milk gently to the boil in a saucepan with the onion and garlic. Cover and simmer on a low heat for 15 minutes.
2 Meanwhile, toast the nuts under a preheated hot grill until evenly golden brown. Rub off the skins and grind to a powder in a coffee or nut grinder or food processor.
3 Remove the onion halves from the milk in the saucepan and discard. Add the breadcrumbs to the milk with the ground nuts and season to taste with salt and pepper. Stir well. Remove from the heat, and leave to swell and thicken for at least 1 hour.

4 Meanwhile, separate the celery stalks and cut into even lengths. Cut each stalk crossways into 2 equal lengths.
5 Steam the celery or cook in boiling water until just tender – about 10 minutes. Do not overcook. Drain well.
6 While the celery is cooking, add the butter to the sauce and reheat gently, stirring occasionally. Check for seasoning.
7 To serve, divide the hot celery between 6 heated plates, arranging it in bundles in the centre of each plate. Pour over the hot sauce.

Breast of pheasant with honey, lemon and caper sauce and chillied parsnip purée

3 pheasants
1.2 litres/2 pints water
1 onion, peeled and halved
10 juniper berries
1 bay leaf
salt and pepper
juice of 1 lemon
30 ml/2 tbsp clear honey
15 ml/1 tbsp capers

25 g/1 oz butter, cut into small
  pieces

The parsnips
900 g/2 lb parsnips, peeled and cut
  into pieces
50 g/2 oz butter
5 ml/1 tsp chilli powder
salt

1 Cut the wings and legs from the pheasants and put aside for another dish. Neatly remove the breasts from the carcasses. Remove the skin and trim away any untidy bits of meat. Reserve the carcasses, skin and meat trimmings. Set the breasts aside.

2 Put the water, onion, juniper berries, and bay leaf in a large saucepan. Add the pheasant carcasses plus all the skin and meat trimmings. Season to taste with salt and pepper. Bring slowly to the boil, skimming off from time to time any scum which may rise to the surface. Simmer for 1 hour.

3 Strain the stock and chill for at least 3 or 4 hours, to allow any fat to rise to the surface and solidify.

4 Remove any fat from the stock. Return the stock to the pan and boil furiously to reduce

to 300 ml/½ pint. Add the lemon juice, honey and capers.

5 Add the 6 pheasant breasts to the pan. Cover and simmer for 15-20 minutes. Remove the pheasant breasts from the stock and keep hot.

6 Meanwhile, cook the parsnips in boiling salted water, or steam until tender – 10-15 minutes. Drain well, then mash or process in a blender or food processor with the butter, chilli powder and more salt to taste to produce a smooth purée. Keep hot.

7 Boil to reduce the stock to 150 ml/¼ pint, then stir in the butter. Check the seasoning.

8 To serve, slice each pheasant breast into 1-cm/½-inch slices and arrange on heated plates. Pour over the sauce. Spoon on some parsnip purée.

Chocolate, orange and tofu mousse

150 g/5 oz plain chocolate
30 ml/2 tbsp water
45 ml/3 tbsp clear honey
grated rind and juice of 2 small
  oranges
400 g/14 oz firm tofu (see page 36)
3 egg whites, whisked until stiff
  but not dry

1 Melt the chocolate in a small heavy-bottomed saucepan with the water over a low heat. Put in the container of a blender or food processor and add the honey, orange rind and juice and tofu. Blend until smooth.

2 Pour and scrape the mixture into a bowl.

Mix in 1 spoonful of the beaten egg white to lighten the mixture, then carefully fold in the remaining whites.

3 Divide the mixture between 6 small serving dishes or glasses. Refrigerate until well chilled.

Left: Crudités with three mayonnaises
Right: Platter of smoked fish with creamed horseradish and pickled walnuts
Below: Aunt Nell's Christmas pudding with brandy butter

Crudités with three mayonnaises

•

Platter of smoked fish with creamed horseradish and pickled walnuts

•

Aunt Nell's Christmas pudding with brandy butter

Crudités with three mayonnaises

*300 ml/½ pint home made or good
    quality bought mayonnaise (see
    pages 20 and 35)*
grated rind and juice of ½ lemon
yellow food colouring
*1 large clove garlic, peeled and
    crushed*
3 anchovy fillets
concentrated tomato purée

*a wide selection of crisp, fresh
salad ingredients, plus raw and
cooked vegetables: wedges of
iceberg lettuce, chicory leaves,
radishes, spring onions, cherry
tomatoes, fennel slices, strips of
red, yellow and green pepper, raw
mushrooms, raw cauliflower florets,
cucumber sticks, celery sticks,
mange touts and stick beans
(blanched for 2 minutes), cooked
asparagus, or anything else that
takes your fancy to add variety of
flavour and texture*

1 Divide the mayonnaise into 3 equal portions.
2 Put one portion into the container of a blender or food processor and add the lemon rind and juice. Blend thoroughly, adding a hint of food colouring to make the sauce a pretty lemon yellow.
3 Blend the garlic into the second portion of mayonnaise, and the anchovy fillets into the third. This third mayonnaise can be coloured a delicate pink by adding a little tomato purée.
4 To serve, place a little pool of each of the three mayonnaises next to each other on one side of each plate. Then add a selection of vegetables, arranging them to show off their contrasts of colour, shape and texture. Offer crusty French bread to mop up the remains of the sauces.

Platter of smoked fish with creamed horseradish and pickled walnuts

175-225 g/6-8 oz smoked salmon,
thinly sliced
275 g/10 oz smoked mackerel
fillet, skinned
100 g/4 oz bottled horseradish
relish

90 ml/3 fl oz double cream,
whipped
2 (150 g/2¾ oz) tins smoked
mussels, drained
6 pickled walnuts, sliced

1 Make small neat rolls from the smoked salmon slices. Cut the mackerel into small equal pieces.
2 Mix the horseradish relish with the whipped cream.

3 To serve, arrange the smoked fish on 6 plates, add a spoonful of the creamed horseradish to each and garnish with slices of pickled walnuts. Offer slices of brown bread and butter.

Aunt Nell's Christmas pudding with brandy butter

100 g/4 oz plain flour
450 g/1 lb shredded suet
450 g/1 lb currants
450 g/1 lb sultanas
450 g/1 lb seedless raisins
575 g/1¼ lb demerara sugar
100 g/4 oz chopped mixed candied
peel
900 g/2 lb white breadcrumbs
grated rind and juice of 1 large
orange
1 good sized carrot, peeled and
grated

1 good sized apple, peeled, cored
and grated
1 whole nutmeg, grated
5 ml/1 tsp mixed spice
5 ml/1 tsp ground ginger
5 ml/1 tsp bicarbonate of soda
4 large eggs
brandy

The sauce
225 g/8 oz unsalted butter
225 g/8 oz caster sugar
45 ml/3 tbsp brandy

1 Place all the ingredients for the puddings, except the brandy, in a large bowl. Mix well, adding a little milk if necessary to make the mixture moist but not wet.
2 Put the mixture into 4 well-oiled medium pudding basins, but do not fill to more than 2.5 cm/1 inch from the top. Cut out circles of greaseproof paper the size of the top of the bowls and place on top of the mixture. Cover the top of each bowl very securely with foil. Steam the puddings for 9 hours.
3 Allow to cool, then remove the covering and douse the puddings with brandy. Cover with fresh paper and foil and store in a cool place, 'feeding' occasionally with brandy, until required.

4 To make the sauce, cream the butter until white, then gradually beat in the sugar. Beat in the brandy a little at a time so that the mixture does not curdle. The brandy butter should now look white and foamy. Pile into a pretty dish and chill until hardened.
5 To serve, re-steam the puddings for 2 hours. Turn out onto a suitable dish. Decorate with holly if liked. Remove any decoration before flaming with warmed brandy if liked. Hand round the chilled brandy butter separately.
Note: Make the puddings at least a month before required. Traditionally, Christmas pudding was made 12 months before eating, and it is certainly true that they improve with keeping.

Above: Sprout timbales with sour cream sauce and julienne ham
Left: Turkey breasts stuffed with chestnuts and vegetables in orange and cranberry sauce
Below: Celery sorbet and Stilton mousse with fruit and nuts

Sprout timbales with sour cream sauce and julienne ham

●

Turkey breasts stuffed with chestnuts and vegetables in orange and cranberry sauce

●

Celery sorbet and Stilton mousse with fruit and nuts

Sprout timbales with sour cream sauce and julienne ham

450 g/1 lb Brussels sprouts,
 trimmed
3 eggs
300 ml/½ pint single cream
salt and pepper

50 g/2 oz cooked ham julienne (see
 page 25)
300 ml/½ pint sour cream (or
 single cream acidulated with the
 juice of ½ lemon, see page 25)

1 Cook the sprouts in boiling water for no longer than 4 minutes. Drain and then plunge into cold water to stop cooking and preserve colour. Drain again well and dry on kitchen paper. Purée in a food mill, blender or food processor (about 450 ml/¾ pint of purée).
2 Beat the eggs and add to the purée with the cream and salt and pepper to taste. Mix together and pour into 6 well-buttered in-dividual moulds.
3 Bake in a bain-marie (see page 24) in a pre-heated 170°C/325°F/Gas 3 oven for 30-40 minutes or until set.
4 Heat the cream in a small saucepan and season to taste with salt and pepper. Do not allow to boil.
5 To serve, loosen the timbales by running a knife around the inside of the moulds, then turn out onto 6 hot plates. Pour the hot sauce around each one and sprinkle with the ham julienne. Thinly sliced brown bread is a good accompaniment to this dish.

Turkey breasts stuffed with chestnuts and vegetables in orange and cranberry sauce

6 turkey breast fillets, each
 weighing 150-175 g/5-6 oz
 (see page 31)
75 g/3 oz butter
1 small carrot, peeled and finely
 diced
1 small onion, peeled and finely
 chopped
50 g/2 oz mushrooms, finely diced
salt and pepper
6 roasted chestnuts, shelled and
 finely chopped

julienne strips of orange rind,
 blanched and drained
 (see page 25)
350 ml/12 fl oz white wine
juice of 1 orange
1 (350 g/12 oz) jar cranberry
 sauce
sprigs of watercress to garnish

The tarts
shortcrust pastry no. 2 made with
 225 g/8 oz flour (see page 20)

150 g/5 oz frozen petits pois
3 small carrots, peeled and finely
 sliced

The bread sauce
6 cloves
1 large onion, peeled and halved
600 ml/1 pint milk
salt and pepper
100 g/4 oz fresh white
 breadcrumbs
50 g/2 oz butter

1 Roll out the pastry thinly and use to line 6 buttered and floured medium patty tins. Bake blind in a preheated 220°C/425°F/Gas 7 oven for 15-20 minutes, or until crisp and pale golden (see page 25). Allow to cool, then remove the pastry cases from the tins and

arrange on a baking tray. Set aside.

2 To make the bread sauce, stick 3 cloves into each onion half and put into a saucepan with the milk and salt and pepper to taste. Bring to the boil and simmer for 15 minutes. Remove the onion and cloves and stir in the breadcrumbs. Remove from the heat and leave to soak for 30 minutes.

3 Meanwhile, trim and flatten the turkey breasts (see page 27). Set aside.

4 Melt 50 g/2 oz of the butter in a saucepan and add the diced carrot. Tightly cover the pan and cook over the lowest heat for 5 minutes. Add the onion, replace the lid and cook for a further 5 minutes. Add the mushrooms and a little salt and pepper. Cover and cook for a final 5 minutes. Tip the vegetables into a bowl, mix in the chopped chestnuts and allow to cool.

5 Stuff the turkey breasts with the cooked vegetables as shown on page 27, and secure.

6 Arrange the stuffed breasts in the bottom of a saucepan which is just big enough to take them in one layer. Sprinkle with a little salt and pepper. Pour on the wine and orange juice. Bring to the boil and allow to simmer for 5 minutes only. Remove the breasts and take out cocktail sticks. Keep warm.

7 Add the cranberry sauce to the liquid in the pan and boil furiously until the sauce is reduced to about 175 ml/6 fl oz. Stir in the remaining butter, cut into small pieces. Keep the sauce hot.

8 Quickly cook the petits pois and sliced carrots separately. Drain well.

9 Add the butter to the bread sauce, stir and reheat. Check the seasoning.

10 Fill the tart cases with bread sauce and arrange the peas and carrots on top. Replace in a warm oven for a few minutes to reheat.

11 To serve, slice each turkey breast into 1-cm/½-inch slices and arrange in a semi-circle on one side of each hot plate. Separate the slices a little so that the stuffing shows. Pour over a little of the hot cranberry sauce and sprinkle with the strips of orange rind. Place a vegetable tart on the other side of each plate and garnish with a sprig of watercress.

Celery sorbet and Stilton mousse with fruit and nuts

The sorbet
1 large head celery, trimmed and
  chopped
juice of 1 large lemon
5 ml/1 tsp sugar
large pinch of chilli powder
salt
1 egg white, whisked until stiff
  but not dry

The mousse
300 ml/½ pint chicken stock
  (see page 19) or water
15 ml/1 tbsp powdered gelatine
225 g/8 oz Stilton cheese
2.5 ml/½ tsp dry English mustard
150 ml/¼ pint whipping cream,
  whipped until thick

1 egg white, whisked until stiff but
  not dry

a selection of fruit and shelled nuts

1 To make the celery sorbet, place the celery and lemon juice in a blender or food processor and blend to a smooth purée. Press through a fine sieve to obtain as much liquid as possible. Discard the solids. Add the sugar, chilli powder and salt to taste.

2 Pour into a shallow container and freeze until slushy but not hard. Remove from the freezer and mix well. Replace and freeze until the mixture is almost solid. Stir well again to break up the ice crystals, then carefully stir in the beaten egg white. Replace in the freezer and leave until 1 hour before required, then remove to the refrigerator.

3 For the Stilton mousse, heat 150 ml/¼ pint of the stock or water until almost boiling. Remove from the heat and sprinkle on the gelatine, stirring until completely dissolved.

4 Place the gelatine mixture, the rest of the stock or water, the cheese and mustard in a blender or food processor and blend until smooth. Allow to cool.

5 Pour the cheese mixture into a bowl and fold in the cream. Fold in the egg white. Pour into a well-oiled small bread tin or other suitable mould and chill until set.

6 To serve, turn out the mousse and cut into 6 1-cm/½-inch slices. Arrange on 6 chilled plates with a spoonful of sorbet and a selection of fruit and nuts. Offer plain digestive biscuits to eat with the cheese mousse.

Above: Mozzarella and Parma ham parcels with fresh figs

Above: Quail tarts with artichoke
soufflés and poached grapes
Right: Orange ice with burnt cream

Mozzarella and Parma ham parcels with fresh figs

●

Quail tarts with artichoke soufflés and poached grapes

●

Orange ice with burnt cream

Mozzarella and Parma ham parcels with fresh figs

3 (175 g/6 oz) packets mozzarella
  cheese
125 g/4 oz Parma ham, thinly
  sliced
3 spring onions with long green
  tops
12 ripe figs

1 Cut the cheese into 12 sticks 7.5 cm/3 inches long, each 2 cm/¾ inch thick.
2 Cut the ham into 12 rectangles, each 13 x 5 cm/5 x 2 inches.
3 Cut 12 long flat strips from the green part of the onions.
4 Wrap each stick of cheese in a piece of ham and tie with an onion strip. About 1 cm/½ inch of cheese should protrude.

5 Slice down through the figs from the tip almost through to the base once, and then again at right angles to the first cut. Open out so that each fig is still joined at the base but the pretty insides of the figs can be seen.
6 To serve, place two figs and 2 cheese parcels on each of 6 plates.

Quail tarts with artichoke soufflés and poached grapes

225 g/8 oz shortcrust pastry no.1
  made with 225 g/8 oz flour
  (see page 20)
6 oven-ready quails
50 g/2 oz butter, cut into small
  pieces
salt and pepper
1 (300 g/10⅗ oz) packet frozen
  chopped spinach
36 green grapes, halved and
  seeded
30 ml/2 tbsp brandy

The soufflés
2 eggs, separated
30 ml/2 tbsp double cream
25 g/1 oz Parmesan cheese, freshly
  grated
salt and pepper
12 tinned artichoke bottoms

1 Roll out the pastry thinly and use to line 6 buttered and floured medium patty tins. The pastry cases must be large enough to accommodate the cooked quails. Bake blind in a preheated 220°C/425°F/Gas 7 oven for

15-20 minutes or until crisp and golden (see page 25). Keep warm.
2 Place the quails in a roasting tin. Dot with the butter and season with salt and pepper. Roast for 25-30 minutes or until the juices run

clear when the point of a knife is inserted into the breast of the birds.

3 Meanwhile, prepare the soufflés. Thoroughly mix the egg yolks with the cream and grated cheese and season to taste with salt and pepper. Whisk the egg whites until stiff but not dry, and fold into the cheese mixture. Place the artichoke bottoms in a buttered dish just large enough to accommodate them in one layer. Spoon the soufflé mixture into the artichokes, heaping it up slightly.

4 Bake the soufflés on a shelf in the oven just underneath the quails for the last 15 minutes of the cooking time.

5 During this time, cook the spinach according to the instructions on the packet. Drain well and keep hot. Poach the grapes in a little water until just hot. Remove the pastry cases from their tins.

6 Remove the quails from the roasting tin and keep warm. Deglaze (see page 25) the roasting tin with the brandy and flambé. There will be very little juice.

7 To serve, divide the cooked spinach between the pastry cases, and place a quail on each. Spoon over the juice. Arrange a tart on each plate with two artichoke soufflés and a few drained poached grapes.

Orange ice with burnt cream

600 ml/1 pint unsweetened orange
*   juice*
2 egg whites, whisked until stiff
*   but not dry*
40 g/1½ oz granulated sugar
5 egg yolks
5 ml/1 tsp cornflour
450 ml/¾ pint single cream
75 g/3 oz soft light brown sugar

1 Pour the orange juice into a shallow container and freeze until slushy but not fully frozen. Remove the container from the freezer from time to time during this process and whisk to mix in the ice crystals as they form.

2 Fold in the beaten egg whites and return to the freezer. Leave until completely frozen, stirring once.

3 Beat the egg yolks with the caster sugar until pale and thick. Mix in the cornflour. Heat the cream to boiling point and pour in a steady stream onto the egg mixture, beating constantly. Strain the mixture into a heavy-bottomed saucepan and place over the lowest heat possible (or over a heat diffuser).

4 Stir the custard constantly until thickened. Do not let the mixture come anywhere near the simmering point or it will curdle. This process could take up to 15 minutes.

5 When the custard has thickened, beat off the heat for a minute to cool. Strain through a sieve into a shallow, flameproof dish. Chill in the refrigerator until set.

6 About 1 hour before serving, transfer the orange ice to the refrigerator to allow it to mellow and soften.

7 Sprinkle the brown sugar evenly all over the surface of the chilled custard, making sure that it comes right up to the edges of the dish. Place the dish under a preheated hot grill and leave until the sugar melts and forms a layer of caramel. Turn the dish if necessary and do not let the sugar become too dark. Allow to cool.

8 To serve, spoon some of the orange ice into 6 pretty dishes or plates. Place a spoonful of the burnt cream next to this, keeping the crispy caramel on top.